SEXUAL SANITY

BREAKING FREE FROM UNCONTROLLED HABITS

Earl D. Wilson

InterVarsity Press
Downers Grove
Illinois 60515

D0052246

InterVarsity Press is the book-publishing division of Inter-Varsity Christian Fellowship, a student movement active on campus at hundreds of universities, colleges and schools of nursing. For information about local and regional activities, write IVCF, 233 Langdon St., Madison, WI 53703.

Distributed in Canada through InterVarsity Press, 860 Denison St., Unit 3, Markham, Ontario L3R 4H1, Canada.

All Scripture quotations, unless otherwise indicated, are taken from The Holy Bible: New International Version. Copyright © 1978 by the New York International Bible Society. Used by permission of Zondervan Bible Publishers.

Cover illustration: Greg Wray

ISBN 0-87784-919-6

Printed in the United States of America

Library of Congress Cataloging in Publication Data

Wilson, Earl D., 1939-
    Sexual Sanity.

    Includes bibliographical references.
    1. Sex—Religious aspects—Christianity.   I. Title.
BT708.W55   1984   241'.66   83-22753
ISBN 0-87784-919-6

17 16 15 14 13 12 11 10 9 8 7 6 5 4 3
98 97 96 95 94 93 92 91 90 89 88 87 86 85

*This book is
affectionately dedicated to my father,
Claude E. Wilson,
who taught me by word and deed
what it means
to be a responsible husband
and father. His life
has truly been an example
of sound judgment and sexual sanity.
Thanks, Dad.*

Preface

Sanity is sometimes defined as sound thinking. In that regard we are all sane, but some of us are more sane than others. The topic of sanity as it relates to sexuality is important to all of us regardless of how we evaluate our current status. The issue is not who is sick and who is well, but how can we all be as sexually healthy as possible. God has allowed me to struggle with this area of my life, and he has allowed me to help others in their struggles. My prayer is that the pages which follow will direct you to wholeness and happiness in your sexuality. God is a giver of good gifts, and it is insane to waste the gift of sexuality.

The book has three main purposes. First, to present human sexuality in a positive light. Sex is good because God has made it good. Second, to present some of the basic problems which arise when our view of sexuality becomes distorted. Sex can be destructive if we make it destructive. Third, to present some practical help for dealing with sexual problems. Sexual sanity can be developed and even restored when it has been lost.

I offer the book to you as a map from a pilgrim to a pilgrim. As it is helpful to you, we will praise God together.

Part I
The Roots of
Sexual Insanity

I
Sanity in an Insane World

THE WILSON CLAN ARRIVED in our hotel room at about nine o'clock, tired from a long day's travel. We decided to relax and watch a little TV in hopes that it would help us unwind. Mike, thirteen, took the responsibility for finding the best show.

We're lucky, we thought. This place has cable TV. We'll have lots of choices. In less than ten seconds, Mike found himself looking directly at a woman's bare breast as she crawled into bed with her lover. He quickly turned the channel as his older sister taunted him. "I'll bet you liked that," she teased.

Obviously, the world of family entertainment has been invaded by overt sexual material. Each member of the family can be directly affected by television, radio and the mounds of sexually-explicit material available on the newsstand of the local market or drugstore. We live in an age in which marketing strategies and motivational schemes are developed to exploit human sexual arousal. Only a few minutes of watching television or browsing at the newsstand makes a teen-ager or adult aware that sex is a powerful force.

Mike will have to personally decide how to deal with overt sexual stimuli. So will his older sister and brother, and so will his younger sisters. We can close our eyes temporarily, but the media's emphasis on sex will not go away. A multibillion-dollar industry is founded on exploiting our God-given interest in sex and turning it into an obsession that the media helps develop and maintain.

As an adult male and a parent, I am aware that sexual temptations are not limited to youth. In God's providence he chose to give us sexuality for a lifetime. As long as we are sexually alive, we are sexually vulnerable.

Is Society Sexually Insane?

Recently a college student told me, "I don't know whether I'm going crazy or not. I can't seem to focus on anything. I don't know how to relate to girls, and I don't know what to do with my sexual thoughts." There is no question about it—it is difficult to live in a society which is insane over sex. Many people have become so unbalanced that they place sex above even their personal safety.

Hardly a day goes by but I hear another sad story of an individual being used or abused by someone who is trying to meet his own sexual needs. Billions of hours and billions of dollars are spent by people trying to get more out of their sexuality or trying to be more sexually attractive. What would modern advertising be without the sexual element? All these factors point to a society in which sex is king. People live for sex. For many people, sex is all there is. It promises everything but often delivers nothing but broken promises and heartache.

We have moved a long way from "doing what comes naturally." We have made sexuality unnatural. It is no longer a normal activity between two people committed to each other, but a production between masked players on a stage. When the masks come off, and they do, who are the people?

If this is not insane, it certainly is absurd. Sex is meant to add flavor and quality to life. This is not what it is currently doing. We have added the whole bottle of seasoning to the recipe of life and are naively asking why it doesn't taste right. Excess creates obsession, not satisfaction.

Webster's Seventh New Collegiate Dictionary defines obsession as "1: a persistent, disturbing preoccupation with an often unreasonable idea or feeling; 2: an emotion or idea causing such a preoccupation."

Much of modern society is preoccupied with sex. Many college students and other adults with whom I talk are highly disturbed by their sexual feelings. They are often experiencing a high degree of sexual arousal and a low degree of sexual satisfaction. Both their emotions and their thoughts are adversely affected. This may be because they are giving sex an unreasonable amount of importance. Sex is a part of our lives. In sexual obsession, however, it becomes the most important part. One young man said, "I think about sex all the time. It is really hard to think about anything else." A female friend said, "I just want that intimacy so badly, I don't know what to do."

Sexual obsession is a form of worship. We give our hearts and minds and bodies in order to remain in a state of sexual arousal. It is one aspect of what Paul talks about when he refers to worshiping created things rather than the Creator.

Therefore God gave them over in the sinful desires of their hearts to sexual impurity for the degrading of their bodies with one another. They exchanged the truth of God for a lie, and worshiped and served created things rather than the Creator— who is forever praised. Amen. (Rom 1:24-25)

People suffer from sexual obsession when sexual thoughts control them rather then being able to control the thoughts.

We all have some areas of obsession whose intensity may vary. Some, for example, are obsessed with diets. These same people are often obsessed with food. Monday night football or soap operas can turn into obsessions. They can lead people into fantasy and delusion.

Many people who would never consider overt sexual action are caught in the trap of sexual obsession. They live in an unreal world of mental promiscuity, trying to fulfill needs through fantasy. I often advise my clients who have trouble dealing with the realities of life to stop watching the "soaps." They need to use the energy they are expending in their fantasy world to help them structure their lives in the everyday world.

Clearly if we are to understand many of the maladaptive sexual behaviors present in today's society, we must have a better understanding of obsessional thinking. Preoccupation with sex can capture us entirely even when we do not consciously want to be captured.

Thoughts that persistently thrust themselves into consciousness against the conscious desire of the patient are known as obsessions. Obsessions persist in the conscious mind so tenaciously that they cannot be dispelled by conscious processes and are uninfluenced by logic or reasoning. The obsessive thought is strongly charged with the emotions of guilt or depression, is unwanted, and usually plagues the individual almost constantly. The sufferer cannot understand why he is obsessed with the thought.[1]

Although I disagree with Kolb's belief that obsessions "cannot be dispelled by conscious processes and are uninfluenced by logic or reasoning," I agree wholeheartedly with his assessment of the severity of the problem. His description matches almost perfectly the mental state of many people I have talked with, people who are heavily involved with pornography or some undesired sexual expression such as uncontrolled masturbation, voyeurism, fetishism or pedophilia. They do not want to continue the behavior, and yet their minds are constantly filled with thoughts of the action. As one person said, "I didn't want to go to the topless bar. I just ended up there."

Christian response to people with sexual obsessions has varied from total rejection and incrimination to total acceptance of both the person and the problem, which is seen as something outside the person—the devil made you do it. Neither approach is very helpful.

In this book I will stress a system of dealing with obsession which is based on personal responsibility and choice. As Kolb suggests, there are no simple solutions. If there were, people would not still struggle with obsessions. It is time, however, that we who are followers of Christ take seriously the battles that rage within, so that we may more effectively bear one another's burdens.

Elements of Sexual Obsession

Three aspects of sexual obsession must be understood by anyone who wants to control this area of life. These are emotional excitement, anxiety and strong reinforcers.

First, sex and emotional excitement have become synonymous in our culture. For many people, sex is excitement and excitement is sex. "Turn on" has other meanings, but its primary application is to sexual arousal. When a person is "turned on" both mentally and physically, obsessional thoughts are strengthened and take more control.

Second, sexual obsession results in anxiety. This is because obsessive thoughts often run contrary to our stated value system. We are anxious whenever we entertain thoughts that oppose our religious or moral beliefs. When this happens, our guilt feelings usually increase and self-respect decreases. As self-respect diminishes, anxiety rises and the probability of seeking comfort through obsessional thoughts increases. Ironically we often seek comfort in what is destroying us instead of in deliverance.

Urgent need also fosters continued involvement with obsession. We are needy people, and one of our great needs is to discover ourselves sexually. Both women and men whose needs for affection are not met may substitute obsessional thoughts. Unfortunately such involvement often leads to greater withdrawal from people and depersonalization of themselves and others.

One young woman said, "I wanted love, but all I got was sex! I sought comfort in masturbation but all I felt was guilt and loneliness." Her two-sentence story shows the dilemma in which people find themselves. Affection needs are not met through sexual obsession.

Why is breaking the sexual obsession habit so hard if obsessional thinking does not really meet our basic needs? The answer is to be found in the third aspect of sexual obsession: powerful reinforcers. Sexual activity usually includes a high degree of arousal followed by release of tension, a very pleasurable pattern for the individual. This keeps people involved in sexual activity even though they may consider it wrong or sinful.

Each aspect of sexual obsession feeds into the others. Excitement strengthens reinforcement but it also increases anxiety. Anxiety may increase excitement, and the release of anxiety becomes a strong reinforcer. Reinforcement increases excitement, but when coupled with guilt it may increase anxiety. It is a vicious circle. Each element of sexual obsession contributes to our loss of control until sanity and rationality are left in shreds.

Elements of Sanity
Sanity returns when three things happen. One, we control our sexual behavior rather than being controlled by it. Two, we use sex for its intended purposes—pleasure and procreation—rather than to meet other psychological needs. Three, we keep sex in its proper perspective and don't take it too seriously.

First, controlling rather than being controlled is addressed in a marvelous statement in 1 Corinthians 6:12. Paul writes: " 'Everything is permissible for me'—but not everything is beneficial. 'Everything is permissible for me'—but I will not be mastered by anything." Certainly sex is permissible, lawful, good, desirable and fun—but Paul recognizes the dangers of being controlled by good or evil. To be controlled by anything other than Jesus Christ is idolatry and therefore sinful. Sex needs to be a part of our lives, not the all-consuming force. When we control sex, it brings peace and calmness along with pleasure.

Some time ago I asked a student friend I had not seen for a while how things were going. His answer shocked me. "Fine," he said, "once I gave up the idea that I had to be a stud." He went on to say that once he stopped living for his sexuality he found that he had a lot more to live for. "I've even gotten interested in the Lord again," he said. It was obvious he was feeling a lot better about himself. Being controlled by sex feels good during arousal, but it usually leaves one subdued and purposeless afterward.

Second, within marriage there are two purposes for sex—pleasure and procreation. Any time sex is used for other than these two purposes, it creeps toward insanity. Jill was eighteen when she first had sex. She didn't intend to, she just got carried away. She also got pregnant. Jim married her to provide the baby with a decent home.

As two kids trying to find out if there was life after marriage they never got very far and their sex life together never developed. Jim's interest waned and he began to spend more and more time at work. Jill was starved not only for sex but also for affection. She began to be attracted to other men and allowed herself to be wooed by them. Each time she had sex, she felt worthwhile. Jill was caught in the trap of proving her worth by being used.

When I first saw her she couldn't figure it out. She had been physically close to men, but she was suffering from the shallowness that sex without emotional closeness can bring. She was teetering on the brink of insanity, ready to take her life. Jill had to learn that she could not find or prove her worth sexually. She had a lot more to offer than her body.

There is a certain type of insanity associated with using sex for other than its intended purposes. I strongly believe that sexual sanity comes when sex is engaged in by a man and a woman who are married and deeply committed to each other. People who engage in sex apart from these constraints run the risk of becoming enslaved to their sexuality and thus having it lose its meaning. This is a waste and approaches insanity.

Third, keeping sexuality in perspective is always difficult. In *The Valiant Papers* Calvin Miller has written of forces in our society which work against a sane perspective on sex.

The entire planet celebrates its common appetite. They make every possible use of this omnipresent urge. Sex sells soap and autos, hand cream, and clothing. From highway billboards half-naked forms, gargantuan in size, gaze out over eighteen lanes of traffic. These titan nudes smile down in bronze skin to sell the products they espouse. Seductive mouths smile with an intrigue across the void, begging tourists to lust, if only for an instant, as they hurtle down the freeways.

SEX, SEX, SEX. It must be said three times to make three syllables. Yet, this silent, screaming inner drive drives men![2] Sex is beautiful. Sex is fun. Sex is a gift from God. However, when sex becomes god, it can become ugly, boring and enslaving. One of the biggest challenges we must face today is the challenge of viewing sex from God's perspective in order to keep it as beautiful and as fun as he intended it to be.

Why do so many people in our culture risk enslavement, meaninglessness and even insanity for the sake of momentary sexual stimulation? In the next chapter we will look at today's crisis in values that leads to such self-defeating behavior. This will be followed by chapters on sexual arousal and obsessional thinking. Part two then discusses common sexual struggles such as masturbation, voyeurism, promiscuity, pornography and homosexuality. Finally, part three gives some specific help in dealing with sexual temptation and overcoming obsessional thought.

2
The Not-So-Modern Crises in Values

SEXUALITY AND GENERAL MOTORS have both been characterized by a philosophy which emphasizes that "bigger is better." The implications for GM and other American automobile manufacturers have become obvious; sales declined and interest in small cars grew. Front-page headlines report multimillion-dollar losses and drastic measures to reorganize to meet current consumer needs. The implications of the bigger-is-better philosophy for human sexuality, although less publicized, may have effects on the individual that parallel those experienced by the massive corporation. What is at stake?

Bigger-Is-Better versus Savoring
Pleasure! In a throwaway society, we are told to grab all the pleasure available from any existing source and then move on to something bigger and better. Any pleasure received is transitory and only helps prepare for the next source of pleasure. We are

taught to take all we can, but never to form any attachments and never to be satisfied with what we have. There is a strong expectation that no one can be satisfied for long by one individual or even a group of individuals. We are expected to be bored, so we must constantly keep our eyes and ears open for the next great opportunity for stimulation.

The constant emphasis is on the green grass on the other side of the fence, and thus the pleasures of our current mate diminish by comparison. Our culture trains men to look for the largest, firmest breasts, the softest hair and the shapeliest buttocks and thighs. The assumption is that these physical characteristics give the greatest sexual pleasures. These attitudes create an atmosphere in which the multibillion-dollar pornography industry can thrive. Without such attitudes, pornography would become boring. The bigger-is-better philosophy, applied to sexuality, has made our society obsessed with sex and pleasure, while millions of people are unable to find in normal human sexual experience the pleasure that God intended.

A number of years ago a noted sports celebrity was arrested for pedophilia (sexual contact with preadolescent children). At the very time of his arrest his wife, with whom he was living, was being featured in a sensuous television advertisement that was attracting male attention from coast to coast. How can a female whose sexual stimulus is so strong that she attracts the lustful attention of millions of males be inadequate to meet the needs of the man who has access to her body? What is the problem here? There is no simple explanation. To say that bigger-is-better thinking causes pedophilia is much too simplistic. The causes of aberrant sexual behavior are often complex.

The illustration does, however, raise a question. When you engage in bigger-is-better thinking, where do you go when you reach the top? What happens to the person who owns a Cadillac but cannot enjoy it because he would rather have a Rolls Royce? What happens to the person who owns two Rolls Royces?

While living in Iran in 1970 I formed a habit of going to a local news agency early Tuesday morning to buy one of the few copies of *Sports Illustrated* that they put on their shelf at that time. Waiting for the packages to be opened, I became aware of the types of literature that were being displayed. A new line of cheap paperback books appeared with catchy but corny sexually suggestive titles and cover pictures to match. One morning I took one of the books and read some of it. It was written at a third-grade level and had little plot. I was shocked to discover that most of its pages were devoted to vivid descriptions of a married man's pursuit of many preadolescent girls. There were details of the pain experienced by the young girls and the pleasure received by the man as he "tore apart the tender hymen." Such nauseating literature promotes bigger-is-better thinking.

People are trained to be dissatisfied with what they have and to look for a bigger thrill in some new sexual experience. Many individuals move from one type of sexual encounter to another: from wife or husband to neighbor's wife or husband, to a woman or man at the office, to group sex, to homosexual encounters, to mixed sexual encounters, and even to encounters with children. It is reasonable to assume that those obsessed with children as sex objects would choose younger and younger children until the child could hardly be seen as a sex object at all. Mohr and Associates reported in 1964 that 4% of pedophilia victims were age 3 or younger, while 18% were between ages 4 and 7.[1] Will the progression continue to the point of total insanity?

As a therapist I have been shocked by the number of physically healthy, sexually attractive people who report that they receive no pleasure from sex or that the pain outweighs the pleasure. If they engage in sexual activity, it is only to meet the sexual expectations of others or to bolster their sagging egos by proving that they can still do it. Men often try to prove their worth through sex. Women are often caught in the trap of feeling obligated. At the same time, they may be looking for some sensational experience such as multiple orgasm. It is little wonder that both men and women come to resent sex. These problems associated with bigger-is-better thinking lead to inability to savor the moment and to enjoy the pleasures of normal sexual activity. Is this dismal state of affairs all life has to offer? Is there a biblical alternative in a throwaway society?

In Search of a Biblical Alternative

Any philosophy of pleasure must allow for the rightful place of pleasure in a person's life. Contrary to the beliefs of many, the Bible indeed recognizes and emphasizes the place of sexual pleasure. Noted evangelist, pastor and writer John Allan Lavender says crisply: "It needs to be said in a Christian context, and not just read on the pages of *Playboy* magazine, so let's say it: Sex is fun! It is a God-ordained, God-blessed means of letting out the child in you, of having fun without feeling guilty or battering the family budget."[2]

The book of the Song of Solomon tells about God's intention for our sexual pleasure. In essence it is the story of savoring what you have as opposed to being obsessed with what you feel you must have in order to be satisfied. I encourage you to read Song of Solomon 4:1-7, where the woman's beauties are savored by her lover, and Song of Solomon 5:10-16, where the woman describes the physical characteristics of her man. The descriptions emphasize the beauty of the human body while illustrating the joys of savoring the person. There is no indication that either person has found the perfect body, but rather that each has found delight in the other person. With glee the woman in love states, "This is my lover, this my friend" (Song 5:16).

A number of years ago a young woman, age eighteen, was referred to me by her pastor. Sue had engaged in sexual intercourse with eight or ten different men during the previous six months. In trying to find the key to her lack of self-control, I discovered that she was actually receiving very limited pleasure from her sexual activities. Sue's primary need was to be accepted by men and to receive affection from them. However, when acceptance and affection were offered she often rejected them. She did not know how to savor the fact that she was accepted.

The way she handled compliments illustrates this. When a male friend said to her, "You look pretty tonight," Sue's internal response was, "If he thinks I look pretty, he would probably like to feel me." She took no time to enjoy the fact that God had given her beauty. She rushed quickly into deeper and deeper levels of sexual involvement, never stopping to enjoy the pleasures along the way. Although she felt guilty because her promiscuous behavior was contrary to her religious beliefs and her personal and family standards, she seemed to be unable to stop it. Sue was a Christian, but she was caught in bigger-is-better thinking. The result was guilt, dissatisfaction and sex without pleasure.

In counseling her I emphasized three key factors: repentance, forgiveness and savoring. The first two were not new concepts; her pastor had adequately covered them with her. The third concept, savoring, had to be learned.

Sue decided to break off all contact with previous lovers and to approach future relationships with men in the new way. Together we pinpointed her needs—acceptance and affection. I encouraged her to look for times when these needs were being met. For example, when a man was showing her attention, she was to remind herself that he was appreciating her and that she was appreciating him. This self-talk helped her to savor each situation without pressing for overt sexual contact which would distract her from meeting her emotional needs. By following this pattern Sue successfully avoided promiscuous behavior and was much happier as she learned to accept the joys in each relationship for what they were rather than always pushing for more.

There is strong encouragement in Scripture to find enjoyment and satisfaction in who we are and what we have without getting caught in the trap of making comparisons with others. Indeed, comparison with others invariably leads to dissatisfaction with what we have. If I spend time appreciating my wife's beauty and her skill in lovemaking, I will grow closer to her and undoubtedly appreciate her more as a lover. The question of whether there are more beautiful women or women more skilled in lovemaking is not the point. Looking for other women or even thinking about that possibility will only lead to meaningless comparisons and dissatisfaction.

Comparisons are bad for a number of reasons:

First, the Bible specifically forbids making comparisons. "Each one should test his own actions. Then he can take pride in himself, without comparing himself to somebody else" (Gal 6:4). "We do not dare to classify or compare ourselves with some who commend themselves. When they measure themselves by themselves and compare themselves with themselves, they are not wise" (2 Cor 10:12).

Second, comparisons are rarely based on reality. The unknown always looks more glorious than the known.

Third, comparisons are often based on outward appearance. They usually begin with visual stimulation. You can't tell what a person is really like just by looking at him or her. If you begin by comparing outward appearances, you may become blind to the inner qualities which are so important.

Fourth, comparisons almost always ignore the human interaction that is all-important in relationships emphasizing pleasure. A man or woman may be beautiful but not right for your personality. Many people become sexually obsessed with individuals that they don't even like. Once the initial excitement has diminished, these relationships often self-destruct. Unfortunately, many such relationships are extramarital affairs which result in divorce, remarriage and divorce. Sometimes it is only after the second divorce that the person realizes what a mistake it was to leave the first relationship.

It needs to be said clearly! Why waste time and emotional energy focusing on what we cannot have at the expense of enjoying existing sources of satisfaction?

I love this story which underscores savoring:

Recently, at a Christian camp, I was talking with a well-satisfied husband who was describing his wife to me. . . . "I can't imagine how any woman could be more exciting in bed than she is. She has learned how to turn me on so easily that it's embarrassing sometimes." It was obvious that he could go on forever. He was happy with her and he was deliriously happy with the marriage. Without thinking, I immediately conjured up in my mind the image of a ravenously beautiful seductress "on the make." . . . Then she walked up, and my images crumbled. She was short, flat chested, and a bit on the homely side. . . . She was his lover, and as she approached you could tell that she was a "beautiful woman." . . . Her beauty depended upon the grace of her person. She felt good about herself inside and whatever she lacked physically the loveliness of her inner self more than made up for it.[3]

To savor is to avoid coveting. To savor is to extract pleasure from present experience. When we savor God, we call it worship. When we savor sex, we call it satisfaction and contentment. Savoring increases pleasure while bigger-is-better thinking leads to despair.

In all fairness to our hedonistic society with its emphasis upon bigger as better, we must say that the Bible recognizes that we can find pleasure by following our fallen desires and instincts. The long-range outlook, however, is not good. The pleasures of sin are seasonal. In Hebrews 11:25 we read, "[Moses] chose to be mistreated along with the people of God rather than to enjoy the pleasures of sin for a short time."

When you view sexual pleasure as temporary and press onward to find more excitement with a bigger and better experience, you are denying what should be the basic emphasis of sexual pleasure —*the relationship*. When sex is separated from a loving, caring relationship it becomes mechanical and mundane. Orgasm without acceptance isn't really that meaningful. On the other hand, knowing that you are wanted and loved can pave the way for a lifetime of sexual excitement. *Only through relationships can long-term pleasure be found.*

Take All You Can Take versus Give All You Can Give

The 1970s have been characterized as the decade of the self: self-improvement, self-help, self-assertion, self-gratification and self-indulgence. These attitudes have affected our sexual practices. Taking care of yourself is good because no one else will take care of you. Obviously, then, in the sexual realm you had better take (for yourself) all you can take. This approach is particularly prevalent among males who are enculturated to go as far as they can go, leaving the female to stop them or to protect herself against the possible consequences.

The values crisis here is obvious. Loving becomes taking! In fact, loving is a misnomer. To have intercourse or to engage in any form of sexual contact without taking into account the other's needs, safety and value as a person is a form of rape, whether the person consents to it or not. The biblical view of sexual activity stresses giving, not taking. Concerning sex in marriage, Paul writes:

> The husband should fulfill his marital duty to his wife, and likewise the wife to her husband. The wife's body does not belong to her alone but also to her husband. In the same way, the husband's body does not belong to him alone but also to his wife. Do not deprive each other except by mutual consent and for a time, so that you may devote yourselves to prayer. Then come together again so that Satan will not tempt you because of your lack of self-control. (1 Cor 7:3-5)

The most notable thing in this passage is its emphasis on providing for the other person. To fulfill your marriage vows is to give pleasure, *not* to rip the other person off. There is no place for exploitation in biblical lovemaking. In the words of Jesus, "It is more blessed to give than to receive" (Acts 20:35).

Sexual obsessions definitely promote a take-all-you-can mentality. Some pornographic materials, for example, stress taking even if violence toward the other person is required. Sex without commitment allows each person to use the other for his or her own pleasure. This often creates an atmosphere of fear of rejection that ultimately destroys the sexual relationship.

The take-all-you-can ethic is also apparent in the modern view of premarital sex. Despite the women's liberation movement, the man is still expected to go as far as he can while the female is expected to stop him or at least to protect herself. I believe that this situation damages the identity and future sexuality of each. The *Kahn Report on Sexual Preferences* published in 1981 cites some of the negative feelings expressed by females about losing their virginity. Sandra Kahn summarizes:

My point here is that even though more and more girls are losing their virginity before marriage, they still carry feelings of guilt and conflict over the "promiscuous" relationships they have during developmental years. The guilt that a woman builds up about sex in her childhood and adolescence usually remains with her through mature adulthood.[4]

Exploitation never leaves people whole. It always leaves them fragmented.

Men, too, are affected by their own exploitative behavior. Many men have the illusion that a normal red-blooded American male should be able to sleep with a different woman every night without experiencing any feelings other than the pleasure of the moment. This may be an appealing theory, but what I hear from many males who have tried to practice this lifestyle is that pleasures diminish while feelings of guilt and dissatisfaction over treating women as subhuman grow. There may be some individuals who are capable of continued sexual exploitation without feeling guilt, but I believe their number is small. Exploitation of others in any form is contrary to God's way. We cannot tamper with God's design without experiencing the consequences.

Another negative effect of taking all you can take is never learning how to give. This results in impoverished sex during marriage and an inability to get close to people emotionally. Respect—for others and for self—is the most important element for relationships, as well as for one's own mental health. Sexual exploitation does not lead to respect in any form.

Using prostitutes is one of the oldest forms of taking all you can take. Although prostitution is illegal in most states, many people consider it acceptable because users of prostitutes at least give something—money—in return. Even this is sexual exploitation because the person is not considered. Most prostitutes are young girls who sell their bodies to survive. Many are involved in the depersonalized world of drugs; many have been kicked out of their homes or have run away, often to escape an incestuous or brutal relationship. Giving money only perpetuates the problem. In fact, payment increases the depersonalization that the woman already feels. Moreover, the person who contributes to another's depersonalization usually feels depersonalized himself. Paul stated, "He who sins sexually sins against his own body" (1 Cor 6:18). The damage inflicted on the exploiter is at least equal to that felt by the one exploited. It may just come in a different form.

When people are asked to list what they want most in life, they do not usually mention sex. They do, however, put love high on their list. Love comes when people give all they can give, not when they take. If the so-called golden rule is followed in sexual practice, it will promote good mental health. If it is ignored, people are destroyed by the sexual expression they crave. Jesus said:

> In everything, do to others what you would have them do to you, for this sums up the Law and the Prophets. Enter through the narrow gate. For wide is the gate and broad is the road that leads to destruction, and many enter through it. But small is the gate and narrow the road that leads to life, and only a few find it. (Mt 7:12-14)

Nonpossessive versus Nondominant Relationships

A third crisis in values results from the modern philosophy that meaningful sexual activity is completely unrelated to any notion of possession. In other words, there should never be sexual jealousy because there is no ownership. Pornographic writers suggest that men and women should freely allow their spouses or sexual partners to have sex with others as they wish without any feelings of personal loss. This point of view is a major thrust of Gay Talese's book, *Thy Neighbor's Wife*. He records comments by Barbara Williamson:

> Most married people, she said, had "ownership problems": They wanted to totally possess their spouse, to expect monogamy, and if one partner admitted an infidelity to the other it would most likely be interpreted as a sign of a deteriorating

marriage. But this was absurd, she said—a husband and wife should be able to enjoy sex with other people without threatening their primary relationship.[5]

The biblical view of marriage clearly contrasts with this position. In 1 Corinthians 7:2-4 Paul writes:

Since there is so much immorality, each man should have his own wife, and each woman her own husband. The husband should fulfill his marital duty to his wife, and likewise the wife to her husband. The wife's body does not belong to her alone but also to her husband. In the same way, the husband's body does not belong to him alone but also to his wife.

In Genesis the purpose of the male-female relationship is to guard against loneliness (Gen 2:18) to promote psychological and physical unity (Gen 2:24) and to produce children (Gen 4:1). I believe that God made us to experience mutual ownership without domination. When I use the term *ownership* I do not mean owning your spouse like you own an automobile. I am talking about a relationship in which the husband can say, "I am hers and she is mine," and the wife can say, "I am his and he is mine."

Ownership is an important element of self-esteem. I must own myself, and I need to find joy in those relationships which are mine. It is important to me as a person to be able to say that this is my wife or that I am Sandy Wilson's husband. I can hardly imagine that self-esteem is enhanced when a man can say, "I am married to that woman who is taking off her clothes and offering herself to Joe Blow."

Ownership, by allowing us to belong uniquely to someone else, makes relationships personal. Lack of domination recognizes the partner as a person, not a thing. Ownership without domination is crucial for feelings of specialness to develop. Sexual stimulation and excitement can certainly be practiced without ownership or with domination, but I do not believe that such sexual relationships can meet a person's basic needs.

Sexual relationships should never be reduced to a produce-upon-demand arrangement. This, too, is damaging to self-esteem, especially the esteem of the person on whom the demands are made. Loving is a caring business, and those who do not feel cared for in love will suffer greatly. On the other hand, people thrive when they know they are desired without being dominated or used to fulfill the spouse's ego needs. I am proud of my wife, and I do not have to dominate her to prove my worth.

Sensuality versus Sexuality

Many Christians blame Sigmund Freud for the current interest in and misuse of sexuality. Freud carefully constructed a theory of personality which gave prominence to the stages of psychosexual development. Freud's emphasis upon sexuality, however, was not the same as the emphasis of many modern writers, even though they may try to give their views credibility by teaming them with his esteemed name.

Sexuality for Freud was not genital. It involved the total person. Freud stressed the role of tension and tension reduction, but he recognized that not all tensions are sexual and that not all are the result of internal stimuli.

Modern society has placed the emphasis on sensuality instead of whole-person sexuality. Sex is viewed as a product of our person rather than an expression of our whole person. The popular media often emphasizes the importance of the skillful, maybe even ruthless, performance of the sex act. Total-person sexuality, on the other hand, involves not just sensuality, but the total realm of feelings about oneself as a sexual being. One view stresses ejaculation and orgasm. The other view stresses love, compassion, sexual excitement and shared pleasure. Lewis Smedes clearly draws the distinction. He writes:

> Our sexuality makes us excitingly sensitive to physical delights in the intimate touching of another person's body. God has made us body-persons finely tuned to pleasure. So, when we talk of sensualism as a distortion of sexuality, it is not the experience of, nor the desire for, sensual pleasure that is suspect.
>
> Sensualism becomes a distortion of sexuality when it cuts physical pleasure in sex off from a personal quest for higher values. It distorts sexuality into a lust for physical pleasure that

dominates one's sexual life. Sliced away from one's total growth into a human being of character, sensual pleasure tends to control our sexual development.[6]

Sexual therapists agree that one of the greatest causes of sexual maladjustment is the unwillingness of sexual partners to take time giving pleasure to each other. One cause of maladjustment is the emphasis on sensuality and sexual climax as opposed to knowing the person, with sexual pleasure flowing naturally from that intimate relationship. Dr. Helen Singer Kaplan writes:

A trustful loving relationship is important to insure good sexual functioning. For a woman, a feeling of trust that the partner will meet her needs, particularly the dependency needs, and a feeling of security that the spouse will take care of her, will take responsibility for her, will not abandon her and will be loyal to her seem necessary in order to enable her to abandon herself to sexual pleasures. In fact, recent evidence indicates that trust may be one of the most important factors determining orgasmic capacity in women.[7]

Clearly, Kaplan's emphasis in sex therapy goes well beyond a preoccupation with sensuality. Such an emphasis does not teach one how to develop a trustful, loving relationship. It can, in fact, destroy our ability to function sexually. What a tragedy that God's great gift, sensuality, can be emphasized until it destroys the very purpose for which it was given—pleasure! The business of pleasure becomes the business of boredom. Sex without pleasure, because of this distortion, reveals the absurdity of the *Playboy-Cosmopolitan* philosophy. John White provides a balanced perspective.

Our first step must be to thank a loving Creator that we experience sexual desire. For not only is physical sex itself ordained by God, the physical pleasures of sex are God-given. Your body has the capacity to be deliciously stimulated because God made it so. Pleasure, as C. S. Lewis once pointed out, is God's invention, not the devil's.

Unfortunately the modern world, like the ancient world before it, has made a goddess of sensuality, worshiping sexual pleasure instead of receiving it with thanksgiving. Men and women have become slaves of lust rather than joy-filled servants of God. And a Christian, reacting to a flagrantly hedonistic culture, may fall into one of two extreme errors. On the one hand he may himself be enslaved and on the other, in his fear of lust, he may deny himself the enjoyment God planned for him.[8]

Sex for Tonight versus Sex for Life

The final values conflict revolves around immediate versus delayed gratification. Grabbing the gusto as quick as you can is pitted against building a solid relationship from which gusto can flow for life. As a parent, I am committed to teaching and showing my children that it is possible for a man to be fulfilled sexually and emotionally by one woman for an entire life. I want them to know that my wife, their mother, is still just as sexually exciting for me as she was when I was first attracted to her at age fifteen. They also need to know that she finds me sexually exciting as we move pell-mell into middle age.

As I mentioned in chapter one, some people believe that the best fruit is forbidden fruit. This denies the importance of relationships in finding pleasure. Delayed gratification is not held in high esteem by the so-called sexually enlightened. It is interesting to note, however, that those who direct their lives to helping people experience sexual fulfillment speak strongly for sex based on strong relationships rather than on casual acquaintance. LoPiccolo and LoPiccolo write: "If a husband and wife spend virtually no time together and have no mutual, shared responsibility for the tasks of day-to-day living, it is unlikely that they will find sex to be a rewarding, close, sharing experience."[9] Kaplan cites fear of failure, demand for performance and fear of being rejected as prime causes of sexual anxiety.[10] All these conditions are likely to occur in a noncommitted relationship. If God intended sexual relationships to be for life, then one cannot expect short-term pleasure-seeking ultimately to contribute to success. The one-night stand, rather than being a cure for personal and sexual ills, may indeed be part of the problem.

3
How We Are Aroused

MANY PEOPLE WITH SEXUAL obsessions—pornography, voyeurism and pedophilia, for example—find sexual arousal in an atmosphere of fear and danger. They apparently enjoy trying new things with new people, believing that arousal can be maintained and boredom avoided only by exploiting the forbidden and the unknown.

In contrast, the biblical view of sexual arousal focuses on safety, security and savoring your lifelong sexual partner. Boredom is avoided because safety and security offer the constant refreshment of a sound, loving relationship. Yet fear does play a role in sexual arousal for some people, and boredom can be a problem in long-term relationships. In this chapter we will look at fear and boredom in the light of biblical guidelines for the fulfilled life.

Arousal Based on Fear?

When I first heard a professor from a prominent Eastern university say that sexual arousal is associated with a perception of fear and danger, I thought he was absurd. As I listened to what he had to say, however, I realized that his theory has elements of plausibility. The late Dr. Hans Selye, the noted physiologist and student of human stress, has helped us to realize that the human body responds to many different stimuli with a state of general arousal. I can feel nervous, for example, and not really know whether I am excited or afraid. My state of arousal may be triggered by many different agents, some of which are pleasant while others are not. I apparently must decide, by a cognitive process, what is causing the arousal so I can respond appropriately.

This analysis lets us see that a person who is aroused by a fearful or dangerous situation may cognitively label the response as sexual excitement. Herb said, "When I go to dirty movies I get sexually aroused long before I get there! The closer I get, the more the excitement builds and builds. I finally reach a point of no turning back." When I asked if he feared being caught, he admitted that he was risking his family, his reputation and his job.

I suggested that he label his two emotions accurately. When he was going to the movies he was to acknowledge his fear and remind himself that it was genuine. But he must stop telling himself how sexually aroused he was unless there was some stimulus for sexual arousal in front of him. This approach worked, and Herb was able to begin to unlock the chains of his obsession.

Although emotion is still not fully understood by psychologists and physiologists, it is clear that emotion involves both physiological components such as hormonal secretions and cognitive components such as labeling the internal experience. For example, a person may look across the street and see the neighbors undressing for bed. Since many people believe that spying on their neighbors is wrong, violating this value may result in an aroused state. A feeling of danger may precede any feelings of arousal. The person may be saying, "I shouldn't look!" But if the person looks anyway, he or she may become aware of bodily sensations. As the couple undresses, the watcher may interpret those bodily sensations as sexual arousal. It may be impossible to say which came first, the fear arousal or the sexual arousal. In fact, the two sources of arousal may have combined to create an unusually high state of arousal.

Some psychologists who work with people who participate in voyeurism (gaining sexual satisfaction by watching others in various states of undress or in sexual activities) believe this combined arousal state may be one reason that voyeurism is so resistant to treatment. In any event, an encounter with a feared or dangerous situation may result in physiological arousal and may be combined with sexual arousal. This phenomenon has been reported by many individuals who found themselves sexually aroused when they were not seeking it. For example, some women who have received obscene telephone calls report that after the call they experienced what they thought was sexual arousal, even though they had been terribly frightened by the caller. Men report that following life-endangering situations they have become sexually aroused without consciously focusing on any sexual stimulus. There definitely is a connection between fear, danger and sexual arousal. The connection seems to be in the way we label our general arousal state.

Fear and danger may also contribute to sexual arousal with unfamiliar persons or events. A man may become highly aroused by seeing a woman other than his wife partially clothed or nude. Even if his wife is physically more attractive, the fact that he is familiar with his wife's body but not the other woman's may affect his arousal state. He may then try to sneak another peek at the other woman, not because he can't keep his eyes off her great beauty, but because viewing her body is forbidden by existing cultural standards. Many men report that they are stimulated by women at topless bars and in X-rated movies, not because of their exceptional beauty, but because they aren't supposed to go see them. Women also report that when they are aroused by men other than their husbands, their arousal does not stem from what is done or said but from their belief that the men are forbidden to them. Seductive or flirtatious behavior is often most effective when it is forbidden. We come to believe that if there is risk involved there must be more value in the interaction.

Sexual arousal may also occur when fear and danger are linked with a remembered sexual event. Dr. Robert Stoller has suggested that sexual perversion may be the working out of fantasies that maintain their importance to the individual because of unresolved childhood conflicts. He writes:

> My hypothesis is that a perversion is the reliving of actual historical sexual trauma . . . and that in the perverse act the past is rubbed out. This time, trauma is turned into pleasure, orgasm, victory. But the need to do it again—unendingly, eternally again in the same manner—comes from one's inability to get completely rid of the danger, the trauma.[1]

The stimulus in this case would be to have the trauma, as relived in the fantasy, come out differently than in the actual experience. A woman who is raped, for example, may be sexually aroused by fantasies of the attack—only this time she fights the person off or becomes the sexual aggressor herself.

Sexual arousal can also be based on fear in normal sexual experience. A man may become aroused just by thinking of asking his wife to participate in some form of sexual activity they have not yet tried. Fear of her rejection may be sexually stimulating or may be interpreted as sexual arousal as he imagines asking her. The mind works in strange ways to interpret the feared situation as highly desirable.

Sexual arousal is highly affected by one's desire for new experience. Dr. Abraham Maslow has listed the need for new experience as a basic human need. In the sexual area this desire is often equated with the forbidden. The clear message of most pornography, for example, is that real sexual satisfaction is to be found by bed hopping. Males are led to believe that if they stay in the same bed too long, they will no longer be able to get an erection. Females are persuaded to meet their desires whenever and with whomever they please. The most arousing sexual partner, according to such literature, is a new partner. Indeed, the natural hesitation and fear of meeting new people may add to sexual arousal.

Thus far we have seen that there are definite connections between fear, danger and sexual arousal. A state of general arousal can result from either fear or sexual stimuli. In fact, a person may interpret fear-based arousal sexually even in the absence of specific sexual stimuli. The combination of sex and danger can create a state of high arousal. But the questions remain, Are fear and danger the only bases for a continued arousal state? Are they compatible with long-term sexual satisfaction? Is there a better way?

Safety, Security, Savoring

I have always been leery of anyone who goes to the Bible to prove specific points that are not explicitly spelled out. The Bible is the great source book on matters of faith and theology, and it has a lot to say about anthropology. However, the Bible is not a handbook of science, although it contains accurate scientific information. Neither is it a psychology or sexology book, although it has many important things to say in these areas. The Bible presents principles that contribute to a sound understanding of sexual arousal. A view that is compatible with biblical teaching must be based on the concepts of safety, security and savoring. The biblical view stands in direct contrast to the fear-and-danger model.

The first clear record of sexual awareness is recorded in Genesis 3. Following their disobedience to God in the Garden of Eden, Adam and Eve became aware of their nakedness. In Genesis 3:7 we read: "Then the eyes of both of them were opened, and they realized they were naked; so they sewed fig leaves together and made coverings for themselves." Later in the chapter, God explains to Eve that "your desire will be for your husband" (v. 16). This may be the first biblical reference to sexual arousal. In Genesis 4:1 we read a simple statement of sexual union: "Adam lay with his wife Eve, and she conceived and gave birth to Cain."

The next biblical reference to sexual arousal is found after the record of the birth of many sons and daughters, grandsons and granddaughters of Adam and Eve. In Genesis 6:1-2 we read:

"When men began to increase in number on the earth and daughters were born to them, the sons of God saw that the daughters of men were beautiful, and they married any of them they chose." This passage would indicate that sexual behavior had gone beyond the bonds of marriage which God intended and had resulted in a type of multiple marriage situation which displeased God. God's response was judgment in the form of a flood.

After the flood, the purified family did not remain pure for long. Ham apparently made fun of his father's drunkenness and nakedness and was cursed (Gen 9:20-25). In Genesis 12 we read the grim account of Abraham's lie. He told the Egyptians that his beautiful wife, Sarai, was his sister. The Egyptian king was sexually attracted to her and added her to his harem. This was a dark moment for Abraham. Years later, after God had drawn up his covenant with Abraham, sexual morality had deteriorated still more. This deterioration is epitomized by conditions in the cities of Sodom and Gomorrah. Lust was rampant and was being expressed both heterosexually and homosexually. Even after the destruction of the cities and of Lot's wife, who looked back, we find incest between Lot and his two daughters.

Personal misuse of sexuality continues. Genesis 39 records the story of Potiphar's wife and her attempted seduction of Joseph. We will discuss this passage in detail in chapter seven as an example of dealing with sexual temptation. Suffice it to say at this point that her sexual arousal was based not on safety, security and savoring, but on desire for the forbidden.

The other side is seen in biblical relationships in which sexual desire is established in marriage and maintained. Even before Ruth and Boaz were married, their attraction for each other was based on kindness and not on danger. In Ruth 2:13-16 we read:

"May I continue to find favor in your eyes, my lord," she said. "You have given me comfort and have spoken kindly to your servant—though I do not have the standing of one of your servant girls."

At mealtime Boaz said to her, "Come over here. Have some bread and dip it in the wine vinegar."

When she sat down with the harvesters, he offered her some roasted grain. She ate all she wanted and had some left over. As she got up to glean, Boaz gave orders to his men, "Even if she gathers among the sheaves, don't embarrass her. Rather, pull out some stalks for her from the bundles and leave them for her to pick up, and don't rebuke her."

The Song of Songs is a biblical model for a relationship between a man and a woman that is highly sexual and very tender. The speakers show deep appreciation for each other's body and for the continued expression of their love. Although the passage is erotic, it is flavored with sensitivity to the person. If you read the Song of Songs while watching an X-rated movie, it would seem out of place. The passage stands as a clear alternative to distorted views of the body and the person. Notice in Song of Songs 4:9-10, "You have stolen my heart, my sister, my bride; you have stolen my heart with one glance of your eyes, with one jewel of your necklace. How delightful is your love, my sister, my bride! How much more pleasing is your love than wine, and the fragrance of your perfume than any spice!" Most people I talk to about their sexual needs long for the type of personal sexuality described in Song of Songs. Unfortunately many are able to find only the type of depersonalized sex that is depicted in pornographic material.

The Bible does not record many statements made by Jesus about sexuality. He spoke out against adultery and fornication in the Sermon on the Mount, and he extended forgiveness and healing to those caught in sexual sin. Although Jesus apparently did not talk much about sexuality, he always had women around him and undoubtedly appreciated them both as people and as sexual beings. Smedes writes:

Jesus did not experience genital sex. But this need not mean that he had no feeling of being a man among women. The differences between male and female did not melt into a vague mass called human nature when he looked at real men and women. He related to women as a male to females. He must have felt the difference between the tender touch of women and the hard handclasp of men. And there is no reason to suppose that he had no erotic feelings toward women, that he never enjoyed the sheer female presence of Mary. Nor is there any reason to suppose that women felt no erotic attraction toward him.[2]

If Smedes's interpretation is correct, then it is obvious that sexual attraction and arousal take place in the context of safety and security such as that which Jesus offered for Mary. The story is beautiful. It is also clear that Jesus' view of sex was very wholistic. There is no reason to believe that his intent was genital. He enjoyed the women because of who they were, not because his purpose was to be aroused.

It is sad that some modern writers insist on going beyond the evidence, insisting that Jesus had to have had genital sexual relationships. The life of Jesus serves as an example of sexual control and appreciation of sex without exploitation. Again I quote Smedes:

What Jesus did for human sexuality was considerable. For instance he treated women as persons equal with men. Running bluntly against both Jewish and Gentile culture, he publicly displayed a tenderness and concern for women that demonstrated his respect for them as persons. He accepted them in his inner circle of friends. He turned against the legalistic double standards of his time by exposing the hypocrisy of the males who accused a woman caught in adultery. He undermined legalistic morality by recalling that the heart has its own kind of sex life. He subverted male arrogance by contradicting the Jewish tradition that approved of the exclusive right of husbands to get rid of their wives as they got rid of their stock. He showed that marriage and sex were planted in the Garden of Eden, reminding us that God intended from the beginning that men and women should be sexually attracted toward each other, and that sexuality therefore was not one of the nasty products of sin but the exciting dynamic of creation (Mark 10:5-9).[3]

Although the Bible gives examples in which sexual arousal may have been associated with fear and danger, the biblical ideal is for sex to be relational, not mechanical. The general patterns for relationships as set forth in Ephesians can serve as a base for lifelong sexual arousal. "Get rid of all bitterness, rage and anger, brawling and slander, along with every form of malice. Be kind and compassionate to one another, forgiving each other, just as in Christ God forgave you. Be imitators of God, therefore, as dearly loved children and live a life of love, just as Christ loved us and gave himself up for us as a fragrant offering and sacrifice to God" (Eph 4:31—5:2).

Novelty and Guilt

Having discussed two possible theories and lifestyles related to sexual arousal, I will focus on two elements that affect sexual arousal: the importance of novel stimuli and the absence of guilt.

Any activity, even sexual activity, can become boring. Paul Hauck writes, "Whether it be listening to great music, eating wonderful food, making love, skiing, or whatever, it is impossible to do anything that one ordinarily enjoys without sometimes becoming bored. Woe to the man who cannot tolerate some boredom, for he shall forever be bored."[4] I believe that sexual obsession can be a response to boredom. A person who is bored with sex because it has become depersonalized may become obsessed with sexual thoughts in hopes that sex will get more exciting. But obsessional sex is always depersonalized, so boredom increases and the obsession grows deeper.

Of course there is a place for variety within normal sexual experience. When sexual activity becomes boring, introducing novel stimuli can make a difference. In working with people with sexual dysfunction, I have found that the range of sexual activity in which these couples engage is limited. Neither partner seems willing or able to introduce new ideas or practices. Although Marabel Morgan has been criticized for suggesting that wives meet their husbands at the door dressed only in Saran Wrap, her idea of novelty is good.[5] Studies of marital sexual adjustment indicate that good lovers like surprises. The same type of excitement that one can have by fantasizing about the neighbor's wife can be had by becoming involved with your own wife if there is novelty in the relationship.

One friend stated his belief succinctly: "The best sex contains novelty, and the best novelty sex can be found within the safety of the marriage relationship." A healthy sexual relationship between two Christians contains the best of both worlds—the freedom to explore and enjoy the erotic domain within the safety of a caring, committed, marriage relationship. The marriage partners are restrained only by their own physical comfort level and their sensitivity to the comfort level of their mate. This attitude can free the couple to learn to be lovers for a lifetime—which, as I read the Bible, is God's plan. Lifetime lovers have the freedom to be creative because of the security they feel. If they fail one day, they have time to try again. This attitude does a lot to destroy the performance mentality which seems to destroy sexual drive as well as sexual relationships.

A second factor that affects sexual arousal is guilt. People who feel guilty about sex do not enjoy sex and are often sexually inhibited. It doesn't seem to matter whether they are Christians or not. One study found that high-guilt subjects could not enjoy viewing pornographic slides. As the sexually explicit content was increased, these subjects tended to spend less time viewing each slide. High-guilt scores tend to suppress sexual arousal in other types of contacts as well. High-guilt persons who are active sexually often report that they are doing more and enjoying it less.[6] In marriage, guilt feelings have been shown to be one of the greatest deterrents to satisfactory sexual adjustment. Helen Singer Kaplan writes:

Some persons are so conflicted and guilty about their erotic needs and desires that they actively discourage their partners from stimulating them effectively. Careful questioning often reveals that such persons respond to sexual excitement by immediately stopping the activity which produced it. The man who is excited by an active and seductive woman may literally forbid his wife to behave in this fashion. The woman who is only responsive to slow tender caresses may push her husband away when he tries to kiss her or to caress her.[7]

I believe that a straightforward proclamation of the biblical view of sexuality can do a great deal to lower the guilt level for many people and to provide greater spontaneity within the marital relationship. Feeling guilty about violating God's standards is appropriate. However, feeling guilty about normal sexual arousal and responses is a serious mistake. We respond to the opposite sex, not because we are abnormal and sinful, but because God made us sexual beings.

A person with a strong moral code related to sexuality must understand that sexuality is good and that sexual expression within God's framework can be great. When we violate the code, God wants us to come to him for forgiveness and wholeness, not to heap guilt on ourselves that prevents us from enjoying his gift.

Parents often cripple their children by seeking to control sexual activity through inducing guilt. It makes more sense to emphasize the positive. Sexual self-control is important because it prepares us to take maximum advantage of what God has provided for our pleasure. Shame does not produce good mental health, good Christian character or good self-control. Sin needs to be addressed again, but it is senseless to produce guilt as a substitute for self-control. Guilt will not inhibit sexual arousal. It will only keep us from using our sexuality as God intends.

We must definitely seek a balance. Shamelessness—total sexual expression without inhibition—leads to boredom and lack of arousal. On the other hand, shaming ourselves or others denies us the joy of celebrating our sexuality. Sex should always be filled with mystery and excitement, not just because sex itself is exciting but because the sexual partner is an exciting creation of God.

4
Obsession: The Vicious Cycle

JOHN IS TWENTY-SEVEN-YEARS old and has been married for six months. He and Judy have had good months as they have begun their life together. They have enjoyed their sexual life thus far except for one major disappointment—John still masturbates. They had assumed that once they married and felt free to express their sexuality fully, John's problem would go away. Much to their chagrin, it still exists. Judy, his wife, feels that she must not be desirable or this behavior would not persist.

John and Judy, however, have an inadequate understanding of the problem. They, like so many others, have the mistaken view that masturbation, voyeurism, use of pornography, and other forms of obsessional sexual behavior are related to pent-up emotional energy or the need for sexual release. In fact, this is not the cause.

John's pattern begins with cruising. He drives up and down the streets looking for some partially clad or especially shapely female who will trigger his mind and begin to stir his sexual fantasies. These fantasies are the most important thing in his life. No matter how often he masturbates or has sexual intercourse, almost every day he finds himself cruising and stirring up the thoughts within. In a two-week period during which his counselor asked him to keep track, John discovered that he had spent thirty-one hours cruising and masturbating. This, he felt, was less time than he spent before marriage and counseling.

The numbers are important only in that they underscore the obsessive nature of the problem. People like John who are caught in the web of obsessive behavior usually find other areas of their lives suffering drastically as they invest hours of time and tremendous emotional energy indulging their fantasy. Much like the alcoholic, those plagued by obsessive thoughts do not intend to harm themselves or others, but nevertheless end up hurting many. Whether or not masturbation itself is a sin, this out-of-control thought life is certainly sinful. The Bible makes it clear that being controlled by anything other than Jesus Christ is sin. Paul wrote, "I will not be mastered by anything" (1 Cor 6:12).

John may believe that his problem is Judy's fault because she isn't more beautiful or more satisfying. Blaming others is easy when people believe that aberrant sexual behavior is caused by a strong sex drive joined with lack of opportunity for socially acceptable expression. This is a lie of Satan. John's behavior is his own responsibility. It cannot be explained by Judy's appearance or sexual expertise. Before marriage John found it easy to blame God for giving him so much libido. After marriage he blames Judy.

People often justify their self-destructive behavior by blaming others rather than facing the issues squarely. The Bible clearly warns us of the need to control our thinking. A person who refuses to heed Philippians 4:8 all too often ends up with some form of obsessive thinking, whether sexual indulgence, paranoia or destructive comparisons with others. "Finally, brothers, whatever is true, whatever is noble, whatever is right, whatever is pure, whatever is lovely, whatever is admirable—if anything is excellent or praiseworthy—think about such things."

Obsessive sexual fantasy is powerful because it is reinforced by both mental and physical stimulation. Sexual fantasy feels good and is available on demand because it does not require the co-operation of another. Unfortunately, it is self-perpetuating because it involves bigger-is-better thinking—the individual thinks that satisfaction depends on having more.

People involved in obsessional behavior often become guilt-ridden and paralyzed by self-doubt. This may lead to withdrawal from society and from loved ones. At the time when the struggling individuals need the love and support of others the most, they often withdraw because of guilt, shame and the compulsion to stir up the sexual fires within. They may even sacrifice family so they can keep chasing the fantasy.

To understand abnormal sexual behavior, we must first remember that it is a product of obsessive thought disorder. It is not always clear which is cause and which is effect. Obsessive thoughts, emotional problems and physical problems are often combined. Second, obsessive behavior is learned and therefore may be unlearned. Third, it is self-perpetuating because of the physical and mental reinforcement involved. And fourth, it is sin and must be recognized as such.

How Do Obsessions Begin?

There are many theories on the origins of obsessive thoughts. Freudian psychotherapists tend to believe that an obsession is an outworking of repressed desires. Lawrence Kolb writes:

> The explanation of obsessive thought is to be found in the activity of the unconscious and of repression. As a defensive device, a guilty anxiety is displaced to an innocuous idea and the anxiety thereby decreased. The obsessive thought which is consciously distasteful may be related to what is unconsciously desired.[1]

Cognitive theorists, by contrast, have suggested that obsessional impulses may result from irrational thinking or philosophic distortions. People may come to believe that they must have or experience the person or fantasy with which they are obsessed. If obsession is a type of impulse control problem, then clearly what people say to themselves about themselves and about their experience with sex and sexually explicit material is key. John T. Watkins proposes that three cognitive patterns underlie most impulse control problems:

(1) Infantilely believing that one has to have what one wants, or infantilely demanding, dictating, or insisting that desires be satisfied at all costs;

(2) egocentrically believing that circumstances must not be difficult and that life should be easy;

(3) believing that any difficulty, delay, or inhibition is too awful to stand.[2]

We will return to Watkins's idea later.

A third possibility is to view at least some obsessional thoughts as a result of Satan's work. Scripture is clear that one way Satan tempts us is to put undesirable thoughts into our minds. The Gospel of Luke records how Satan worked in Judas's betrayal of Christ. "The chief priests and the teachers of the law were looking for some way to get rid of Jesus, for they were afraid of the people. Then Satan entered Judas, called Iscariot, one of the Twelve. And Judas went to the chief priests and the officers of the temple guard and discussed with them how he might betray Jesus" (Lk 22:2-4). Job also was clearly tempted by Satan as God allowed. The story recorded in Job 1:8-12 should serve as a grim reminder to Christians of the nature of the battle we are in.

The the LORD said to Satan, "Have you considered my servant Job? There is no one on earth like him; he is blameless and upright, a man who fears God and shuns evil."

"Does Job fear God for nothing?" Satan replied. "Have you not put a hedge around him and his household and everything he has? You have blessed the work of his hands, so that his flocks and herds are spread throughout the land. But stretch out your hand and strike everything he has, and he will surely curse you to your face."

"The LORD said to Satan, "Very well, then, everything he has is in your hands, but on the man himself do not lay a finger."

Then Satan went out from the presence of the LORD.

Jesus himself experienced Satan's working on his mind. In Luke 4:3-12 Satan suggests Jesus turn stone into bread to satisfy his hunger after his forty-day fast in the wilderness. Satan then offers Jesus rule over the whole world if Jesus will worship him. Finally he tells Jesus to jump off the Temple and let the angels save him to prove he is God. Jesus dealt with each temptation by reaffirming the truth of Scripture. He resisted by filling his mind with truth rather than with Satan's lies. This is a sound principle for avoiding or overcoming obsessions. We will discuss it more in chapter eight.

Overcoming obsessional thinking means striking a balance. Satan's work is a fact. Our own evil predisposition is also a fact. We must not get so busy blaming Satan that we fail to take responsibility for our own evil bent. Blaming Satan can itself become an obsession if it takes the place of allowing the Holy Spirit to give us control of our own behavior. Notice Jesus' words, "What comes out of a man is what makes him 'unclean.' For from within, out of men's hearts, come evil thoughts, sexual immorality, theft, murder, adultery, greed, malice, deceit, lewdness, envy, slander, arrogance and folly. All these evils come from inside and make a man 'unclean' " (Mk 7:20-23).

The Bible discusses three sources of evil: the world, the flesh and the devil. Each of these three sources of evil may lead to obsessional thinking. Our minds and emotions are affected by worldly philosophies, our own desires and the devil. We need to be alert in each area.

Learning Obsessions

We have all heard or seen something and then not been able to get it out of our minds. Such a seed thought resembles the beginning of an obsessional thought pattern. An obsession develops through the following seven stages:

1. A thought stimulator is present.

2. The thought is pursued.
3. A belief about the thought is formed.
4. A filter develops to interpret life from the perspective of the belief.
5. Actions are generated by the belief.
6. The actions reinforce the belief.
7. Obsession is complete.

In the development of an obsession, a seed thought that may result from any form of sensory stimulation is pursued: The person follows it up so that it can happen again. If the original stimulus is visual, pursuit involves taking another look. If it is physical, pursuit involves touching again or seeking to be touched. If the seed thought was stimulated by a song or a record or a picture in a magazine, the person may purchase the item to have it handy. Each time a seed thought is pursued, it becomes stronger and involves more aspects of the person.

Pursuit of the thought leads to stage three, the formation of a belief such as "I must experience this"—what Watkins calls "infantilely demanding, dictating or insisting that desires be satisfied at all costs." This belief about the thought leads to the development of a filter which ensures that all future input from the environment is interpreted from the perspective of the belief. Just as a camera filter keeps out certain light while accentuating other light, the mental filter controls your perception of events. Filters negate certain features of the situation such as danger or possible negative consequences while they accentuate positive aspects such as the perceived desirability of the experience.

An aspect of the filtering process is *labeling*. When my behavior gives me positive feelings, I may begin to label myself in terms of that behavior. For example, if I enjoy a few concerts I may label myself a music lover. If I do not like the concerts I may say I'm not musical. The interesting thing is that the label controls my subsequent behavior. If someone asks me to a concert I may say yes because I have labeled myself a music lover, not because I like the group that is playing. Labels we give ourselves related to sexual obsessions may be similar. Labels like "I can't control it,"

"I'm always horny" and "I have strong needs" are common. These labels result from previous positive feelings, and they also support our continuing involvement in the obsession.

Filters may be used to exclude certain sexual behaviors. Heterosexuals usually have a filter which says, "I am not aroused by persons of the same sex." Homosexuals usually have a filter which says, "I am not aroused by persons of the opposite sex." The terms homosexual or heterosexual are labels for the filters we develop. My own labels, for example, say I am male, heterosexual and easily aroused by females. Imagine that as I am turning down the parkway on a sunny afternoon I see a slender jogger in the distance. As I get closer to the jogger I realize that I am sexually aroused. The jogger has more and more of my attention and I become more aroused. As I get even closer something happens. I notice that the jogger has hairy legs. As I pass I look into the rearview mirror and see that the jogger also has a goatee and is flatchested. Suddenly I realize I am no longer sexually aroused. My filter says I am not sexually aroused by males.

Filters work for us as well as against us. For example, I have a filter that prevents me from being aroused by children. Unfortunately some people have developed filters that say they are aroused only by children. One strong objection to pornography is that it can cause us to develop filters that are incompatible with socially or scripturally approved sexual expression. I am not saying that use of pornography always leads to sexual crimes, but that the filters we develop in response to pornography lead to sexual frustration and preoccupation in areas where the only outlet is through fantasy and depersonalized sex. This is detrimental to existing relationships and to the persons themselves.

The fifth stage in the development of a sexual obsession involves action. As a person grows to believe that he cannot live without seeing sexy movies, he will find ways to see them. A married man may have a filter that says, "I'm more aroused by movies than by my wife." As he goes to more and more movies (actions based on the thought), both the belief and the filter become stronger. Many with whom I have worked report that this happens even though they become bored by the sexually explicit material. In other words they continue to act on their thoughts even though the material observed excites them less. Under these conditions they maintain their behavior only by their belief and their filters. In turn, as they act on their thoughts, their beliefs are heavily reinforced either by arousal or by sexual release through masturbation. These reinforcers are very strong (strong enough to withstand boredom) and cause the person to become heavily invested emotionally in the obsession. Many men report that they spend more time thinking about the sexual obsession than about anything else.

It is easy to see why positive reinforcement strengthens the action, and action strengthens the belief. It is easy to see why obsessions tend to be self-perpetuating. Obviously, if this process is to be reversed, thoughts and filters must be changed and reinforcers must be controlled. In chapter eight I give specific suggestions on how to accomplish this.

Self-Perpetuation
We have said that obsessions are self-perpetuating—they tend to grow stronger each time the action is repeated. Even boredom isn't strong enough to interrupt the obsessional cycle. In fact, boredom itself stimulates bigger-is-better thinking, which leads to an expansion of the obsession to new areas. When people manage to eliminate boredom by expanding the scope of their obsession—by seeing an XXX-rated movie, for example, they reinforce both the action and the underlying thought. The trap gets tighter.

Obsessions are also self-perpetuated by the belief that control is too difficult or that delayed gratification is too hard. These beliefs become filters which strengthen the obsession. Watkins illustrates this point with a fictitious person named Tom. Comparing Tom with a person not troubled by out-of-control impulses, he writes:

Tom's course of development seems to have gone in a different direction. He too begins by experiencing many desires and demands for immediate gratification. However, Tom continues to function at the infantile level in that he operates *as if* his wants were organismic needs demanding to be met. He develops little tolerance for delay in gratification or for substitute satisfactions. Tom's desires take on the urgency of a screaming 3 month-old, lying rigidly on his back, beet-red, thrashing the air with his arms. He thinks he *has* to have what he wants *when he wants it* and, furthermore, that it is *too awful to stand* when he does not get what he wants. Tom has *low frustration tolerance* in that his impulses and desires are experienced as urgent and compelling. He goes through life insisting that the environment and others gratify his urges.[3]

Many mistakenly feel that the way to deal with an obsession that is just starting is to get it out of their system. This does not work. It only leads to deeper and deeper levels of frustration. The more we think about an obsession, the more it controls us. Yet as physicists have pointed out, no action is totally self-perpetuating. Energy is always lost, and it must be replaced for the momentum to continue. The same is true with sexual obsessions. The only way to control them and to keep them from being self-perpetuating is to cut off the energy supply—in this case, the thought process. Obsessions cannot be burned out. They have to be starved.

The False God

I strongly believe that sexual obsession is sin and must be treated as such. Those who are caught in obsession may feel this is harsh and leaves them with no hope. Allow me to clarify my position. I believe that the sin is not in the sexual activity alone, but also in the type of thinking that supports it. A person whose mind is controlled by obsessional thoughts is committing idolatry as well as sexual sin, since to be controlled by anything other than Jesus Christ is to worship a false god. In 1 Corinthians 6:12-13, Paul wrote:

"Everything is permissible for me"—but not everything is beneficial. "Everything is permissible for me"—but I will not be mastered by anything. "Food for the stomach and the stomach for food"—but God will destroy them both. The body is not meant for sexual immorality, but for the Lord, and the Lord for the body.

John's story at the beginning of this chapter shows the power obsessional thinking can have. It is hard to find time to worship God when you are spending over fifteen hours a week worshiping the idol of sexual obsession. To those caught in this dilemma Jesus says: "Come to me, all you who are weary and burdened, and I will give you rest. Take my yoke upon you and learn from me, for I am gentle and humble in heart, and you will find rest for your souls. For my yoke is easy and my burden is light" (Mt 11: 28-30). Sexual obsession is truly a burden. It is a great weight crushing the shoulders of the afflicted. It is made even heavier if we ask God to bear it for us for a time and then take it back from him. When we do this, guilt is magnified. Our only hope lies in God's readiness to forgive and forgive and forgive.

Many people despair because they repeat their sin. God does not despair. He repeats his forgiveness. (The problem of recurring sin will be discussed in detail in chapter nine.) Do not allow Satan to render you hopeless and helpless by getting you to focus on your sin. This will only lead to greater obsession. Advice from Hebrews 12:2-3 is your greatest help at this point: "Let us fix our eyes on Jesus, the author and perfecter of our faith, who for the joy set before him endured the cross, scorning its shame, and sat down at the right hand of the throne of God."

My purpose in this chapter has not been to discuss solutions. I have reserved the last three chapters for that. I have, however, pointed out that God stands beside us. He is ready to forgive and longs to be in our thoughts. Trust in God's love gives us courage. In Isaiah 26:3-4, we read: "You will keep in perfect peace him whose mind is steadfast, because he trusts in you. Trust in the LORD forever, for the LORD, the LORD, is the Rock eternal."

Part II
Common
Sexual Struggle

5
Masturbation,
Voyeurism,
Promiscuity

IN PART ONE I POINTED OUT how our sexually explicit society can lead to thought patterns which take control of behavior. These obsessional patterns often lead to sexual practices that cause feelings of frustration and guilt. In this chapter I will discuss three common sexual behaviors which trouble many people, showing how each is maintained by obsessional thought. These three are masturbation, promiscuity and voyeurism. I focus on these three behaviors because they are so widespread, but what I have to say can apply to other sexual abuses related to obsessional thinking, such as transvestism, pedophilia and fetishism, as well. I call these "sexual abuses" because they are potentially harmful to individuals and to society, and because they are often out of control.

My basic assumption is that no Christian is to be controlled by anyone or anything other than Jesus Christ. If a sexual behavior (or any behavior) leads one away from Christ, it is to be avoided. My aim is to help readers put more of their lives under Christ's control and thereby gain greater sexual freedom.

Masturbation

Recently I was helping a couple with their sexual adjustment. As I interviewed the wife, I asked if she masturbated.

She responded, "What is that?"

I calmly said, "Masturbation is stimulating your genitals with your hand or some other object in order to feel pleasure or experience sexual release."

She blushed, took a quick breath and said, "Oh, my gosh, if I did I would never tell anybody."

Her response is typical of many Christians. Masturbation is a private practice and many people don't want to talk about it or read about it. People often masturbate as a habit without considering whether or not the habit is in their best interest.

During our next session, my client said, "I've been thinking about the question you asked me last week." I looked puzzled and she said, "You know, the one about M." I nodded and she went on, "I've been thinking about that and I decided I do it." She looked away but I could tell she wanted to see my response. When she saw that I was not going to condemn her, she began to relax. Later she said, "I knew men did that, but I had never really acknowledged that women—even myself—also do it."

McCary summarizes the data regarding frequency of masturbation as follows: "The incidence of masturbation to the point of orgasm among men is generally fixed at about 95% of the total male population. . . . According to the figures of several investigators, 50%-90% of all women masturbate at one time or another in their lives, whether or not they are aware of it."[1] Because masturbation is practiced by such a large percentage of the population, it obviously needs a Christian evaluation. Is it a good practice or not? Does it violate biblical teaching on sexual conduct?

Historically, society has attempted to control masturbation

through scare tactics. Young people who were beginning to explore their bodies were told that masturbation would lead to disease or insanity or impotence. In a lighter vein threats of warts or other disfigurements were common. This type of approach is not completely dead, but few argue today that masturbating has any negative physical effects on an individual.

What about psychological effects? In working with people who are experiencing psychological and spiritual distress, it is often hard to determine whether masturbation produces spiritual and psychological problems or whether spiritual and psychological problems (such as insecurity, guilt, fear and depression) result in masturbation. It seems to work both ways. Overconcern about masturbation and inability to fully accept God's forgiveness may lead to depression. On the other hand, a person who feels insecure or depressed finds it easy to seek solace through masturbation. This may lead to a cycle of guilt-depression-masturbation-guilt, a cycle that is extremely harmful because it offers no hope. I believe that masturbation must be taken seriously, but some people take it so seriously that it becomes an obsession.

I am not arguing in favor of masturbation as a common practice, nor am I suggesting that we take lightly the fear and guilt that often accompany masturbation. But masturbation must be evaluated in relation to our total sexuality. A simple act of masturbation in and of itself may be neither helpful nor harmful. The value or harm may occur from the way in which masturbation fits into the individual's total thought pattern.

Does the Bible Speak about Masturbation?

Masturbation, like many other topics of great personal and social concern, is neither condemned nor condoned in Scripture. In fact, I have not been able to find any direct scriptural statements about masturbation. Christians have not always been honest about this fact and have tried to give the impression that their opinions on the subject were fortified with biblical imperatives. Such is not the case. Genesis 38:8-10, used by some Christians to condemn masturbation, clearly refers to using coitus interruptus as a means of disobeying the levirate marriage law. The issue is not the evil of masturbation but the evil of disobedience and unwillingness to follow God's plan.

Thus, except for its stress on the importance of obedience, this text gives no perspective on masturbation. The Roman Catholic Church has taken a strong stand against masturbation and other forms of sexual activity which deny the possibility of conception. This approach to sex considers masturbation to be terrible not because it is condemned by Scripture but because it is so far removed from procreation. Both masturbation and involuntary nocturnal emissions were condemned by the early church:

> The very word masturbation means "self-abuse," and does not describe the act itself, but is a value judgment upon it. By a curious reasoning, masturbation was deemed an offense more serious than incest, adultery, or seduction by use of violence. And the reason? Because it was an ejaculation of semen furthest removed from the possibility of procreation![2]

Once again, any direct scriptural basis for such an attitude is missing. Therefore we must apply some of the general principles of Scripture to the issue of masturbation. Right thinking, I contend, is the basis for right acting. So let's consider those principles which stress self-control and good human relationships.

In 1 Corinthians 7, Paul talks about passion and self-control. He concludes that people should marry rather than burn with passion: "Now to the unmarried and the widows I say: It is good for them to stay unmarried, as I am. But if they cannot control themselves, they should marry, for it is better to marry than to burn with passion" (vv. 8-9). This seems like a drastic statement coming from one who felt so strongly that marriage hampers the performance of the ministry of Jesus Christ. Paul recognized that not all people had the same type of self-control that he had. Thus he wrote in verse 7: "I wish that all men were as I am. But each man has his own gift from God; one has this gift, another has that." Paul could have suggested masturbation as an alternative to burning with passion. After all, the issue seems to be pleasure or expression of libido rather than desire for the marriage relationship. From strictly a time perspective masturbation isn't incompatible with carrying on a ministry. It takes little time and puts no restrictions on busy schedules. Why wouldn't masturbation have been a better choice than marriage?

One answer seems quite obvious: masturbation is not a means of self-control. It is often a lack of self-control. Sexual fantasy and masturbation allow a person to engage in mental sex with numerous people. This does not seem compatible with Paul's exhortation to have self-control which we read about earlier in 1 Corinthians 6:12-13.

The Issue of Control

I believe Paul might have argued that masturbation, even if permissible, is not beneficial because it is often incompatible with self-control. Further, I believe that to become obsessed with the practice of masturbation is to commit idolatry, to serve a master that is not God. Masturbation may be helpful. Indeed, it is necessary for some couples in order to achieve maximum sexual adjustment. The issue is what or who is in control.

We kid ourselves when we say we can't live without masturbating. That very statement borders on obsession. We need to face the fact that we are a pleasure-loving people and that masturbation is one way we choose to worship pleasure rather than God.

If you masturbate, I do not believe you need to condemn yourself. What you probably need to condemn yourself for is spending more time masturbating than you spend praising God. The issue of self-control and correct priorities is more important than debating whether or not masturbating is a sin. Norman Geisler states:

Masturbation is sinful (1) when its only motive is sheer biological pleasure, (2) when it is allowed to become a compulsive habit, and/or (3) when the habit results from inferior feelings and causes guilt feelings. Masturbation is sinful when it is performed in connection with pornographic images, for as Jesus said, lust is a matter of the interests of the heart (Matt. 5:28). Masturbation can be right if it is used as a limited, temporary program of self-control to avoid lust before marriage.[3]

The uncontrolled practice of masturbation, or any other habit, undermines confidence and can make one despair of ever achieving self-control. You come to believe you can't stop. This sabotages our faith. Some people would quote Philippians 4:13 as follows: "I can do everything except stop masturbating through him who gives me strength."

There is a second obsession associated with masturbation. That is the obsession to quit. People with this obsession, in most cases, are worshiping the creature (themselves and their ability to conquer) more than the Creator. How would you feel if your best friend spent more time thinking about conquering masturbation than he or she spends thinking about you? Do you think God enjoys being in that position?

People do not stop masturbating because of how hard they try. They stop because they focus on something more exciting, the Person of Christ. So you slip and rub yourself. That is no excuse for avoiding God. If it is sin for you, accept his forgiveness and rejoice in your relationship with a Person who can forgive.

Let's keep masturbation in proper perspective. It can be an opportunity to learn self-control. If we are controlled by it, however, we need to be careful not to allow Satan to use that as a wedge between us and God. John White writes:

Your view of the seriousness of your problem is exaggerated. If you search the Scriptures, you will find a lot about virtues God commends to you and sins he warns you about. How do you measure up to them? How about forgetting *your* problem and taking the commands of Scripture seriously? You hurt no one but yourself by masturbating, but whom have you hurt this week by your sarcasm, your coldness, your forgetfulness, your laziness, your lack of tact and courtesy? How many minutes have you praised God in the last twenty-four hours?[4]

Masturbation and Intimacy

A second problem related to masturbation is depersonalization. We live in a paradoxical time. Interest in physical intimacy is at an all-time high, but it is often expressed without regard for psychological intimacy. Frequently, sex is not a person-to-person but a genital-to-genital activity.

John White has cleverly referred to masturbation as "sex on a desert island." If one of God's purposes for sex was to counteract loneliness, then masturbation contributes to the problem, not the solution. When I do sexual-adjustment therapy, I ask, "What do you think of when you masturbate?" The answers are revealing. People rarely think of a warm, psychologically close, emotionally intimate experience. Instead they think of nothing but the friction or just a picture of a nameless person. One man said, "None of my sex objects have faces." It is little wonder that loneliness persists. But when sex is depersonalized, orgasm electrifies but never satisfies. White writes:

This is one of the reasons that masturbation never really satisfies. Orgasm is a small part of a greater and more personal whole. You may not (as John Donne affirms) *be* an island, yet in a sense you are living on an island alone. Your sexual longings are associated with a deeper need—that someone should share your island and bring your isolation to an end. You are frustrated as you pace its length and breadth. The empty seas are about you, and the breakers crash lifelessly upon the sand. Your eyes ache for the sight of smoke on the horizon, and your ears ache for the music of human speech. Masturbation is to be alone on an island. It frustrates the very instinct it gratifies.[5]

Most people do not need to masturbate. They already know they can reach orgasm. Neither do they need to masturbate to experience sexual relief. In fact masturbation creates more sexual tension than it relieves. The more you masturbate, the more you are obsessed with masturbation, and then you lose control over masturbation in a sea of obsessional thinking. If you currently masturbate, let me suggest that you abstain from the habit for one month. If you do, you will probably find that you can do without masturbation altogether.

Many people masturbate because they haven't learned that they can be accepted sexually. But masturbation is not a road to acceptance. Sexual acceptance begins by establishing psychological contact with members of the opposite sex. It happens with clothes on—not off. We need to affirm one another as desirable people, not just as faceless bodies. Our Christian society would be much healthier if we were warm and affirmed the desirability of others while also being responsible enough to keep sexual contact for marriage alone. This is the unique place where general attractiveness can be expressed in a personal way. In discussing why she stopped masturbating, Mary Stewart concluded: "I wanted God's Spirit more than I wanted transient physical titillation, and over and above that, I began to see that abstinence made sense in terms of optimal preparation for *real* sharing with a *real* person."[6]

Millions of people desperately need other people. They need to know that God has made them sexually acceptable, whether or not they could be featured in *Playboy* or *Playgirl* magazines. They find this affirmation through close social contact. Unfortunately, many who need people the most withdraw from social contact because they fear someone might guess that they masturbate. The more they withdraw, the greater the likelihood that they will continue to masturbate. Thus the cycle of loneliness and depersonalization continues. With God's help we need to break down these barriers and relate more openly with one another.

Voyeurism

When the terms *voyeur* or *peeping Tom* are mentioned, people automatically think "pervert." Even though our society condones a wide range of sexual expression, we tend to become fearful and condemn anyone who watches others for sexual pleasure. Voyeurism is an unwanted and often unknown invasion of our privacy. I am concerned about it for three main reasons: first, most people practice voyeurism in one way or another; second, voyeurism is a prominent example of sexual obsession; and third, voyeurism leads to depersonalization of sexual activity.

Recently I shocked my psychology students by saying that one reason we may have chosen to work with people is that we have voyeuristic tendencies. Some people were immediately offended while others nodded their heads, understanding what I was saying. All of us are curious about other people. We are constantly invading others' privacy. In most cases we think nothing of it. At one level sexual curiosity is no different from any other form of curiosity: we like to know about others.

Most people outgrow this curiosity or at least keep it under control. Some, however, become obsessed with a need to see others' bodies or to see others engaged in sexual activity. This obsession leads people to take great risks and do things they would not normally do. Voyeurism as an extension of children's curiosity is natural, but if it becomes a sexual obsession, it can be highly dangerous.

Christians must ask what effect this lifestyle has on the total Christian life. I may not be led to commit rape by looking at a copy of *Playboy* or by watching my neighbor's wife sunbathe in her bikini, but what does the continued practice of voyeurism do to my thought life? Jesus warns against the dangers:

You have heard that it was said, "Do not commit adultery." But I tell you that anyone who looks at a woman lustfully has already committed adultery with her in his heart. If your right eye causes you to sin, gouge it out and throw it away. It is better for you to lose one part of your body than for your whole body to be thrown into hell. And if your right hand causes you to sin, cut it off and throw it away. It is better for you to lose one part of your body than for your whole body to go into hell. (Mt 5:27-30)

The word *lustfully* is best interpreted "intending to lust after her." The usual intent of voyeurism is to indulge lustful thoughts. You cannot stop the thoughts from occurring but you can choose not to indulge them. Close the door of your mind so that these intruders have to leave. Voyeurism throws the door wide open to temptation. This is why it is an unhealthy practice and must be dealt with as sin if we take Jesus' words seriously.

Voyeurism then is one form of sexual obsession. Voyeurs have gone beyond curiosity. They live for the opportunity to see someone's nude body or to watch sexual activity. Each attempt to watch others strengthens their obsessional thinking. Voyeurism, like masturbation, is unhealthy because it is not under self-control or under the Holy Spirit's control. In 1 Corinthians 10:31 Paul admonishes us: "Whether you eat or drink or whatever you do, do it all for the glory of God." Believing that voyeurism in any form can be done to the glory of God is difficult if not impossible.

The last reason for avoiding voyeurism is that it depersonalizes sex and thus contributes to feelings of loneliness and isolation. Voyeurs are possibly the loneliest people in the world. Wanting to be received and welcomed, they feel only shut out—always on the outside looking in. What is needed is less looking at people and more interacting with them. There is no substitute for a good solid heterosexual relationship which reinforces the worth of a person.

Promiscuity

Our sexually explicit society has set a standard of sexual practice for males which emphasizes quantity rather than quality. Many men and some women have come to believe that they are not really sexually mature unless they have had sex with many, many people. According to James L. McCary,

> Promiscuity is generally defined as the participation in sexual intercourse with many people on a more or less casual basis. A person whose own sexual activity is limited in frequency and restricted in expression tends to condemn the more liberal sexual behavior of others as promiscuity. Thus the term is often used more as a derogatory evaluation than as a widely recognized scientific or sociologic label.[7]

Promiscuity can become a sexual obsession. For many people, sleeping around has become a way of life. Some justify the practice by saying, "It's available, so why deprive yourself?" Others tell themselves, "I must find release."

One woman used the analogy of herself as a gift. She said, "At first it felt good to have someone open the package. I enjoy giving. But there was never any permanence. And each time it was given back to me, the wrapping was just a little more tattered and messed up."

The desire for sexual pleasure and the desire for physical closeness are both God-given. The problem is not desire. The problem is figuring out how to meet those desires in a lasting and healthy manner. God's plan is to do this through marriage. Promiscuous relationships may provide pleasure, but they rarely develop self-control or lead to feelings of closeness.

One college student told me, "I really felt it was okay. We were both adults and he really loved me. I believed this with my whole heart. Until, as he slipped off my blouse, he called me by the wrong name."

A young man said, "I don't want to just have sex. I want to feel good about myself. The more I have sex, the more I realize I feel worse rather than better."

Promiscuity does not promote self-worth and strong relationships. Mary Stewart writes:

Feeling isolated has little to do with whether or not one is sharing a bed with someone, or even trying to share a life. I cannot count the nights I have lain awake, sometimes muffling sobs in a pillow, beside a satiated, soundly sleeping male, wondering why I was feeling so alone. It was not that the men in question were doing all the taking and not giving—I did not specialize in relationships like that. Mostly they were people who themselves wanted a real and pretty total relationship. But somehow, just because we were trying to get it all from each other, we ended up having less than we started with, feeling only constraint instead of communication. Somehow we were running the relationship on the wrong fuel.[8]

In the 1970s we heard a lot about the importance of sexual experience as a safeguard against sexual incompatibility. Some argued that the crux of sexual-maladjustment problems was naiveté. This emphasis, coming during the "if it feels good, do it" era, prompted many to abandon their previous views and pursue sexual freedom. Was the experiment successful? No! I see many people coming out of that period who did it more and enjoyed it less. Promiscuous sexual behavior, like masturbation or voyeurism is a dead-end street. It is enjoying the pleasures of sin for a season (see Heb 11:25).

The Bible clearly shows that God's ways are not our ways. We tend to choose destructive roads while God encourages us to walk in the path of life. Part of God's plan is that we might enjoy our sexuality for a lifetime. Obsessional thinking, as it is lived out in promiscuity, masturbation, voyeurism and other sexual abuses, works against this goal.

Proverbs 5 contrasts promiscuous sex with the joyful experience of "drinking at one's own spring." In summarizing the condition of the one who refuses God's way, Solomon concludes: "He will die for lack of discipline, led astray by his own great folly" (Prov 5:23).

God calls us to new levels of discipline and self-control. He also enables us to reach his goals for us. This is a real cause for rejoicing.

6
Pornography and Personal Identity

PORNOGRAPHY CONTRIBUTES TO sexual insanity two ways. First, it may create an obsession in which a person lives to read or watch sexually explicit material. Second, it may fuel other obsessions such as masturbation and voyeurism.

Pornography is geared to create a fantasy world for the participant. Its pictures and stories present a world that naive or unsuspecting people may not have considered before. It is the mythical world of the totally sensuous woman or the supremely virile man. Each page is designed to lead people to believe that the next page will present the ultimate body. Each picture of intimacy is focused to capture people's attention only momentarily before speeding them on to the greatest sex show of all. The reigning sex god is strong enough to enslave worshipers for a moment, but it is too weak to withstand the charms of the bigger and better sex god on the next page, in the next frame.

What happens to the person who runs from picture to picture or from story to story trying to find the ultimate god? My experience with clients caught in the pornography trap suggests an answer.

The Comparison Mentality

Pornography slaves develop a comparison mentality which causes them to be dissatisfied with the current picture, the current story or the current personal relationship. The greatest dissatisfaction, however, comes with self.

If you are caught in the pornography trap, you will grow to believe that you, as an individual, cannot possibly measure up to the sex gods you regularly view. You will come to devalue your own body and your level of sexuality, and this is tragic. As a result, you may become afraid of living in the real world.

For example, Jim, age twenty, is well built and well groomed. Women find him attractive. He would have no trouble getting dates, but he doesn't ask. He doesn't believe he is acceptable physically, and this self-devaluation makes him afraid of getting to know women. He says he hopes to find the right one and marry her, but he won't take the risk even of a close friendship. Instead, he retreats to the unreal world of pornography where he imagines himself a sexual hero.

His success, however, is short-lived. Down deep he knows it is only a fantasy. By comparing himself with the men in the stories, he creates a deeper layer of fear. Really believing that he is unacceptable, he has no place to turn except to another story. He now searches vainly for hope. Temporarily he finds it in stories of the sexual exploits of persons he judges less attractive than he is. He tries to climb back to acceptability by stepping on their backs. The problem is that he doesn't really believe they are less favored. They must have more experience or money than he does. In a matter of minutes, Jim is trapped again. His only alternative is to turn another page.

There is another side of the comparison mentality of which

Jim may not be aware. His experience with pornographic material may be causing him to develop a nonaccepting attitude toward the normal female physique. He may begin to look for goddesses in the real world, just as he turns page after page to try to find them in his fantasy world. He slowly but surely loses touch with reality as he becomes increasingly dissatisfied with himself and with every woman he meets. Pornography has made him dissatisfied with the beauty of God's creation.

People who have developed the comparison mentality will not be satisfied with normal beauty. They will constantly wish for larger breasts or better formed sex organs, not realizing that what they have is all that is necessary for sexual satisfaction. The comparison mentality sets them up for rejection, beginning with self-rejection and then leading to the fear of being rejected by others. Many people get so engrossed in making comparisons that they ignore beautiful people with great potential for love and marriage. They also ignore their own potential and retreat deeper into the fantasy world of pornography.

Performance-Based Sexuality

A second effect of pornography is to establish a performance-based view of sexuality. Both the comparison mentality and the performance expectation lead to self-rejection and fear of being rejected by others, one on the basis of physical attributes, the other because of inability to perform up to the fantasy standards of pornographic stories. Combined, these two traps create feelings of total inadequacy, hopelessly trapping their victims with no alternative but to retreat to more fantasy.

Psychologist Rollo May has spoken out sharply against this emphasis on sexual performance.

It is not surprising then, in this preoccupation with techniques, that the questions typically asked about an act of love-making are not, Was there passion or meaning or pleasure in the act? but How well did I perform? Take, for example, what Cyril Connolly calls "the tyranny of the orgasm," and the preoccupation with achieving a simultaneous orgasm, which is another aspect of the alienation. I confess that when people talk about the "apocalyptic orgasm," I find myself wondering, Why do they have to try so hard? What abyss of self-doubt, what inner void of loneliness, are they trying to cover up by this great concern with grandiose effects?[1]

The person who chooses to live in the fantasy world created by sexually explicit material will invariably become fearful of not being good enough. Performance-based living is a curse in all areas, but it is especially devastating in the sexual area where the standards for success are unattainable.

Our society's strong emphasis on technique in sexual performance has lured many young people into the sexual arena prematurely because of their need to be assured that they can perform adequately. I once debated a liberal theologian who argued that college students should have premarital sex to establish their sexual identity and to find the type of partners with whom they are sexually compatible. In essence he was saying, "Prove that you are a sexual performer and you will feel better about yourself." But what does being a sexual performer mean? If it means fitting sexual organs together, there is little need to prove one's mechanical skills. God has made people so that the organs fit. Fewer than one-half of one per cent of sexually incompatible couples have problems with the physical aspect. Most marriage counselors would agree that the majority of cases of sexual incompatibility are caused by the fear of failure resulting from a high emphasis on sexual performance.

Writers of sexually explicit "love" stories emphasize pleasure and performance rather than the person's well-being as the goals of lovemaking. These standards are devastating, especially to those who take pornographic material seriously. Performance anxiety may destroy not only the ability to make love but the person as well.

Rollo May writes:

A knowledgeable medical student, one of whose reasons for coming into analysis was his sexual impotence, had a revealing dream. He was asking me in the dream to put a pipe in his head that would go down through his body and come out at the other end as his penis. . . . His symbol is remarkably graphic: the brain, the intellect, is included, but true symbol of our alienated age, his shrewd system bypasses entirely the seats of emotions, the thalamus, the heart and lungs, even the stomach. Direct route from head to penis—but what is lost is the heart.[2]

Performance-based living, whether in the sexual or any other area, results in great dissatisfaction. It also results in the erosion of the person. You are more than how you perform. You are created in the image of God. Do you dare define yourself only in terms of your accomplishments? Can your ego stand the performance pressure that you put on it?

You are created in God's image, and he gave you your sexuality as a gift. You do not have to prove that you can use your gift better than anyone else. Gifts are not for competition. They are for enjoyment. Unfortunately, if you allow pornography or any other influence to cram you into the performance mold, you will never enjoy the gift.

We mentioned earlier that the comparison mentality feeds fear of rejection. Performance expectation also causes fear to grow. Performance-based living fosters fear of failure. When you see your sexuality only from the performance perspective, you fear that you cannot perform well enough.

Paul Hauck shows how these fears may affect a person's behavior. He writes:

The fear of rejection and the fear of failure were combined in a most unique way in the case of Rose, who was laughed at sarcastically once during the sexual act with her husband. Thereafter she turned very cold toward him and simply could not perform spontaneously. The marriage eventually ended in divorce, but her fear of rejection and failure hung on with such tenacity that she could not relax even in the company of other men, for fear they too might laugh if she allowed herself to become intimate and romantic. It baffled her that she was so cold, since she wanted very much to permit herself to get close to some of the men she knew. However, it was not until she recalled the incident of being laughed at by her husband that she realized how hurt she had been and how she had let that foolish behavior on his part upset her for a period of about ten years.[3]

Many young people are overcome with fear before they ever get to marriage. I believe that use of pornography contributes directly to these fears. Pornographic material sets a performance expectation that is unreasonable because it is unrealistic. The most devastating material may not be hard-core pornography, but widely accepted sexually explicit materials such as supermarket novels, many modern movies or magazines like *Cosmopolitan*. These materials are seen by many so-called normal people who feel that they reflect normal sexual expectations. Unfortunately they do not.

The Forbidden

Use of pornography perpetuates the feeling that only forbidden things are sexually satisfying. Pornographic material is not designed to help you fantasize about your spouse, but about someone else's spouse, or about children, or about someone of the same sex, and so on. Pornography creates an obsession for the forbidden. It always suggests that what you don't have is better than what you do.

I am amazed at the increasing number of Christian men I see who, by the time they marry, already assume that their wives will not be able to satisfy them sexually. This becomes a self-fulfilling prophecy. If these men are not satisfied, it is because satisfaction is subjective. They have been trained to devalue the socially and biblically acceptable pleasures that are available in favor of the forbidden and the unknown.

If sexuality must be faceless or unfamiliar to be pleasurable, the person has been damaged. There is no hell like the hell of dissatisfaction—refusing or being unable to find pleasure in the marriage relationship which God created for our pleasure. An increased desire for the forbidden—fostered by pornography, among other things—has led to a quest for new types of sexual experience. Increased social problems result as individual moral standards are eroded by the desire for new experiences.

A missionary recently sat in my office telling me of his struggle with lust. He appeared to be doing nothing to enhance his sexual relationship with his wife, but he had begun to fondle his son for the pleasure he could derive from that. His desire for the forbidden had blunted his conscience.

When people say yes to what they know is wrong, they begin to lose contact with reality. A type of spiritual and psychological dualism is created in which beliefs lead to one set of behaviors—living as a happily married person—and emotions lead to another set—pursuit of the forbidden. I discuss this phenomenon in detail in my book *The Undivided Self*.[4] Suffice it to say that people who live in this kind of dualism are so guilt-ridden that they can't enjoy pleasure from any source. They are caught in their self-made trap. Unfortunately when they attempt to escape they often only escape to more forbidden ground. This, of course, is what pornography is designed to promote.

Increased Guilt
The fourth effect of pornography, at least initially, is to create intense guilt. This is particularly true with professing Christians or others who have grown up with a value system that prescribes a narrow set of sexual behaviors. When people do what they believe to be wrong they feel guilty. When people feel guilty their behavior often deteriorates. They will either not function well personally or not relate well with others. No amount of rationalization will cause the problem to go away. Guilt is a reality. Dr. Karl Menninger makes this point clear. He writes, "Has the reader dismissed the whole sin-and-guilt business from his mind? Can he? And the anxiety and depression also? Just call it existential, do you, and plod onward? If so, congratulations. Some of us can't do that. It is a burning sore, a deep grief, a heartache for many of us."[5]

Modern evangelists of a sexual freedom suggest that we handle guilt by creating a new order of sexual behavior in which traditional social mores are either ignored or redefined. Such concepts as trial marriage (living together without being married) and open marriage are offered as modern-day solutions permitting expression of sexuality outside the traditional marriage vows. Great claims have been made for the success of these ventures, but I question the evidence. In *Thy Neighbor's Wife,* Talese chronicles the lives of many who have been heavily involved in pioneering social changes that promote sexual freedom. One of those he writes about is Arlene Gough. Her story ends with a simple explanation.

Arlene's name was in the newspapers: She had been found dead at home in bed with a bullet in her body. The police also discovered lying dead next to her, her lover, a young newspaper reporter employed by the Los Angeles *Times.* On the table downstairs was a recently fired .38 caliber revolver. Within hours the police had arrested, and charged with the double murder, Arlene Gough's sixteen-year-old son.[6]

This doesn't sound like success to me.

Guilt is a real psychological phenomenon. It is powerful enough to alter the basic human personality. If there is no God, then guilt can easily be explained as a socially induced condition which can be controlled by changing the social mores. If, however, there is a God and he has made us to respond to certain built-in needs, such as the need to belong uniquely to someone, then all attempts to stamp out guilt feelings will fail. If God, the Creator, has established guidelines for sexual expression and relationship patterns, then it is easy to see that people who choose to violate those guidelines will experience dissatisfaction and guilt. Pornography's answer is to capitalize on the dissatisfaction and to encourage people to go more deeply into the realm of fantasy and the forbidden to achieve greater personal pleasure. Christians are being brainwashed by modern literature into accepting this philosophy without evaluating the inconsistency in their thinking.

As a therapist I have found that guilt over sexual behavior is a common cause of mental disturbance. Many who are active in the type of sexual life promoted by pornography seem to have lost something. The more sexually active they are, the less they enjoy it! One person lamented, "I seem to be dying inside." My thoughts went to James 1:13-15: "When tempted, no one should say, 'God is tempting me.' For God cannot be tempted by evil, nor does he tempt anyone; but each one is tempted when, by his own evil desire, he is dragged away and enticed. Then, after desire has conceived, it gives birth to sin; and sin, when it is full-grown, gives birth to death." Guilt creates a kind of living death which affects the total person.

Decreased Self-Concept

Another effect of pornography is to undermine self-esteem or decrease one's self-concept. Why do people sneak into X-rated theaters or hide dirty books under their mattresses? Why are pornographic materials sent in plain brown wrappers? We are ashamed! We do not want others to know that these things are a part of our lives.

Is this just because we are not yet liberated? I think not. One young man said to me, "I damaged myself quite a bit by spending so much time in topless bars and X-rated movies." He was aware that his behavior had lowered him in his own eyes. People who live in the unreal world of pornography and sexual fantasy sometimes find it difficult to accept themselves in the real world. They are plagued with fears and guilt which undermine self-acceptance. Conversely, people with low self-esteem may turn to pornography in an attempt to bolster their sagging self-concept. But what they had hoped would be a cure ends up adding to the problem.

Rollo May has discussed the negative effects of what he calls "the new puritanism." By this he means the belief that it is immoral not to express your libido. He writes: "I define this puritanism as consisting of three elements. First, a state of alienation from the body. Second, the separation of emotion from reason. And third, the use of the body as a machine.[7]

The three elements of the new puritanism all have a negative effect on self-concept. Body and spirit or mind must be united, not alienated. Reason and emotion should provide a check-and-balance system enabling people to make good choices. The body is not merely a machine, but an integral part of a person.

Pornography also affects the self-concept by causing us to believe that sex is all that is important. Thus when I am not feeling attractive or virile I may become depressed instead of realizing that my sexuality is only one aspect of my total person. Sex is a part of who I am, but it is not my total person. Increased attention to sexuality which ignores other aspects of the person leads to decreased self-esteem.

Ken grew up in a decent middle-class home where he acquired a strong work ethic and came to value being dependable and trustworthy. Ken ignored his sexuality during his high-school years because he was always busy, conscientiously doing what needed to be done. A casual dater, he never got heavily involved with girls. By most standards he would have been considered sexually naive.

When he entered college he was teased for his sexual aloofness. Women offered to show him a good time, and male friends pressured him to "get it on." Ken felt overwhelmed by the gap in experience and awareness which he perceived between himself and the college crowd. He really didn't want people to know where he was, but the constant pressure was creating an intense desire to understand his sexuality better. "How can I ever catch up?" he thought to himself.

One evening Ken's friends asked him to go to an XXX-rated movie with them. Ken went, not knowing what to expect. He was shocked at first, then uneasy and finally bored. He was glad the theater was dark. After this experience, Ken found himself going back alone. He didn't necessarily want to but he was drawn by the explicit sex. He also explored other areas alone, sneaking to a topless bar or an adult bookstore when he thought he wouldn't be seen. This became his way of catching up. He became less involved in school activities and less dependable. Reluctantly he admitted to himself that he was slipping, losing control—but he couldn't stop.

Ken's self-concept was sagging because of his deceptive life-style and his increasing lack of dependability. At the same time he realized that all his experience with the flesh market was not helping to give him confidence with women. He was coming to view sex as performance, and he was firmly trapped by feelings of inadequacy. He was mired in comparisons and soundly beaten by guilt. He couldn't even remember the ways his female friends had tried to affirm his masculinity. Ken had sacrificed all that he was on the altar of obsession with what he couldn't have. His fantasy life was costing him everything including his self-esteem. He teetered on the brink of despair until he finally grew desperate enough to seek professional counseling.

Ken never intended to get where he was when I first saw him. He didn't even like the movies. They were an insult to his intelligent mind. Why then did he keep going back to be bored? Whatever possessed him to buy all those magazines? Why did he keep going to see plastic people showing off scarred and tattooed bodies? Because he had abandoned the battle for self-respect, preferring to live in the twilight zone of sexual obsession.

Obsessional Thinking: The Crux of the Matter

We have now come to the major issue: Using sexually explicit material leads to being controlled by the fantasies and obsessions which the pornography industry seeks to create. Ken's story shows the type of instability that results from surrendering to obsession with pornography. Although Ken's problems may have been present long before he turned to sexually explicit material, they became more ingrained as he got more involved in pornography.

People who are struggling in this area often describe their behavior as temporary insanity. Clearly if we are to understand many of the maladaptive sexual behaviors present in our society, we must have a better understanding of obsessional thinking and the ways it is promoted.

When Paul writes of his personal struggle with sin he doesn't sugar-coat it. In agony he cries "What a wretched man I am! Who

will rescue me from this body of death?" (Rom 7:24). He answers
the question himself in the next verse—"Thanks be to God
through Jesus Christ our Lord!" (v. 25).

I firmly believe that deliverance from sexual obsession cannot
take place apart from God's help. I am not, however, suggesting
that God is a pill which can be taken as a magical cure. Deliverance
is closely coupled with obedience and a willingness to make hard
choices. A hard choice for some people may be not to use pornography. And this choice may have to be made over and over again
until the old behavior patterns are replaced by new sane habits. In
this we all need God's enablement. He wants our cooperation.

7
Homosexuality

IN THE PAST DECADE THE TOPIC OF homosexuality has jumped from the closet to the headlines. The gay rights movement has become a strong political force which, in part, has encouraged the development of a counter group—the Moral Majority. Unfortunately, the battle lines have been drawn. I say "unfortunately" because I have friends on both sides who are dedicated Christians seeking to find God's will for their lives and genuinely wanting what is best for others.

During the last five years I have counseled a number of Christians (both male and female) who are struggling with problems resulting from same-sex preference. In this chapter I want to share what I have learned in hopes that it will help you better understand your own struggles or the struggles of others.

In my judgment, homosexuality follows the pattern of thinking common to all sexual obsessions. Homosexual lust is basically no different from heterosexual lust. All lust is out-of-control thinking. When I listen to the anguished account of a person struggling with homosexual temptation, I see both the depth of the struggle and the commonality between it and other forms of temptation.

In Romans 1 where Paul discusses human depravity and God's judgment, he mentions homosexuality as one of the practices which God abhors. In Romans 1:26-27 he writes, "God gave them over to shameful lusts. Even their women exchanged natural relations for unnatural ones. In the same way the men also abandoned natural relations with women and were inflamed with lust for one another. Men committed indecent acts with other men, and received in themselves the due penalty for their perversion." In verse 21 Paul outlines the crux of the problem. He writes: "For although they knew God, they neither glorified him as God nor gave thanks to him, but their thinking became futile and their foolish hearts were darkened."

The Bible clearly states that the practice of homosexuality is sin, just as the practice of heterosexuality outside the marriage relationship is sin. We err if we deny this biblical teaching, just as we err if we set homosexuality up as some type of special sin which God judges more harshly than other sins.

Some well-meaning people in and out of the gay church hold that Romans 1:26-27 means that someone who is "naturally," from birth oriented as a homosexual, should not give up his or her "natural" homosexual relations for "unnatural" heterosexual ones. Paul is therefore only condemning homosexual *lust* and *promiscuity* but not homosexual *love* and *fidelity*. But as David Field points out, "Paul is not referring to individual men and women *as they are*. His canvas is much broader. He takes his argument back, far more radically, to man and woman *as God created them*. By *unnatural* he means 'unnatural to mankind in God's creation pattern.' And that pattern he clearly understands to be heterosexual."[1]

As Christians, our purpose is not to condemn but to offer hope. We know that there is hope for every person who wishes to change, because 1 John 1:7 clearly states that "the blood of Jesus, his Son, purifies us from every sin." I am not talking about immediate transformation. Seldom have I seen this happen. I am talking about developing a new set of filters which say, "I can be aroused by persons of the opposite sex."

To explore this possibility, we will first define the problem in terms of behavior patterns. Next we will look at causes of homosexuality. Third, we will analyze same-sex preference as a learned phenomenon. Fourth, we will give suggestions for relearning or learning opposite-sex preference. Finally, we will point to the church as a redemptive community for those who suffer from obsessional thinking in this area.

Definitions and Distinctions

As a conference speaker, university and seminary professor, and practicing therapist, I have become acutely aware of the large number of people who are silently suffering because they do not understand their own sexuality. Many Christians have heard the term *latent homosexual* and agonize over the possibility that it may describe them. I have helped many work through their sexual identity until they find relief from this concern.

Mary Sue, for example, didn't understand her sexuality. Twenty-two years old, she had never had a steady or close relationship with a man. She was attractive, musically talented and fairly athletic. She came to see me after realizing that she had a strong need for affection and physical contact. Having been sexually aroused after spending some time with a female friend, she was terrified that she might be lesbian. Because of her so-called lack of success with males and the intensity of her feelings for her friend, she assumed the worst.

After exploring her situation in depth, I was able to assure her that she was not going to turn homosexual. In fact the evidence indicated that, when given the opportunity, she was quite responsive to males as sexual beings. What she needed to understand was the relationship between sexual arousal and the need for affection and acceptance. Attracted to her friend because she met her needs for acceptance and affection, Mary Sue was surprised when I asked her why she expected not to be aroused in that kind of close relationship. Attraction to a person of the same sex and even arousal in the presence of this person do not constitute homosexuality, latent or otherwise. Mary Sue was experiencing *sexual attraction to a person of the same sex,* which is far different from homosexuality. Later experiences in dating helped Mary Sue realize that her response mechanisms were intact and that she indeed was normal.

I define homosexuality as being sexually aroused or choosing to pursue sexual arousal with members of the same sex *to the exclusion of* sexual interaction with members of the opposite sex. Sexual arousal is common in emotionally intimate relationships where acceptance and affection are expressed. In most cases, however, it is filtered out by our beliefs that we cannot or should not be sexually responsive to someone of the same sex. Thus it does not develop. Same-sex responsiveness is neither unusual nor abnormal. It does, however, need to be controlled.

The major criterion I use for evaluating sexual preference is the stimulus which most frequently arouses the person. Rarely is a person equally aroused by either sex. Even bisexuals seem to have a preference. I always ask people what type of fantasies they have and what type of contact usually arouses them.

Some people may be sexually active with a same-sex partner without being homosexual by my definition. Rex was such a person. He first came to me for counseling because he had been caught having sex with another male in a public rest room. He was engaged at the time, and his arrest caused quite a stir. From the beginning he insisted that he was not a homosexual. As I listened to his story in detail, I believed him. All of his sexual fantasies were opposite-sex oriented, and he was readily aroused by females. Rex was not a homosexual, but he was obsessed with sexual pleasure.

He had been trained by his Christian parents to abstain from sexual contact with females. To touch a woman, he believed, was truly a violation of God's plan. This taboo coupled with his strong sexual drive had driven Rex to an unusual belief: since sex with females was wrong, he assented to sex with males because "that wasn't real sex." He had become a pleasure-seeker, not a homosexual.

I concentrated on helping Rex deal with his pleasure seeking and took the risk of telling his fiancée that I did not consider him a homosexual. After much prayerful consideration she married Rex, and to the best of my knowledge he has been able to escape his pleasure seeking and take pleasure in life with his wife. He has chosen to enjoy what is his rather than chasing fantasies. I must caution that this is a rare situation. Extreme care should be taken to understand in depth any potential marriage partner who has had same-sex experiences. If the person is consistently aroused by the same sex and not by the opposite sex, this will create undue problems for the marriage. Such marriages should not take place without professional counsel and assurance of God's leading.

Thus far we have looked at two persons with opposite-sex preference in spite of their same-sex behavior. What about individuals whose preference seems to be for persons of the same sex? There are at least two types of people who fall into this category: people with homosexual tendencies and practicing homosexuals.

People with homosexual tendencies seem to be aroused by those of the same sex and not by those of the opposite sex. For whatever reason, however, they are not acting on their urges. Although they may masturbate using thoughts of a same-sex person as a stimulus, their filter which says "I am a homosexual" may be weak because of lack of actual experience. Some people in this category are able to relearn sexual preference rather quickly because their options are still open.

As a college student, Jennifer had homosexual tendencies. She had grown up with a strong fear of men and had never experienced tenderness from a man. She considered herself unattractive to men because she had never been close to one. The only psychologically intimate contacts she had ever had were with females. She discovered her own sexual feelings almost by accident, her first sexual thoughts being associated with a female friend.

I encouraged Jennifer not to worry about being a homosexual, but rather to concentrate on getting to know some men well enough to be comfortable with them. This began her process of relearning. As she became more relaxed around men she began to realize that they were a sexual stimulus for her. Her filter which said "I am aroused only by females" dissolved, and she eventually married and adjusted well in her heterosexual role.

I believe the wrong type of experiences could have strengthened Jennifer's same-sex-preference filter. If she had been rejected or abused by the men she was getting to know, she would no doubt have found females even more attractive. By treating members of the opposite sex with honor and respect, we may help provide the atmosphere in which sexual conflicts can be resolved. Mistreatment will surely have the opposite effect. As Christians we have a responsibility to give all we can give, rather than following the world and taking all we can take.

In the other category of people with same-sex preference are practicing homosexuals. These people have a filter which says, "I am aroused by persons of the same sex, and I am not aroused by persons of the opposite sex." The filters are strongly in place. When Christians with same-sex preference are obsessed with or controlled by sexual desires, they usually face a conflict in values. How can they live with the sexual pressure when there is apparently no hope for relief? Paul stated that if Christians cannot control their sexual desire they should marry: "But if they cannot control themselves, they should marry, for it is better to marry than to burn with passion" (1 Cor 7:9).

The option of marriage, however, is not acceptable to a homosexual believer. To live in a sexual relationship apart from marriage is clearly sinful. What is a practicing homosexual to do?

Brian's situation underscores the dilemma. Brian came to see me at the insistence of a friend who noted that he had been acting strange. He was staying out late almost every night, and his desire for God seemed to be waning. Although it was extremely difficult for him, Brian finally admitted to me that he had decided—without his friend's knowledge—to practice his homosexuality. He said, "I decided my desire was too strong to be controlled, and because I couldn't look forward to marriage as a relief I just gave in." My heart went out to this young man. He felt completely defeated and yet saw no other options.

Practicing homosexuals have only three options: to follow their desires, to control their desires or to change their orientation (and opinion is divided as to whether change is possible). A person who believes that it is wrong to practice homosexuality is faced with learning either strong self-control or opposite-sex preference. Those who choose either of these options are to be admired and supported, not feared or rejected.

A word must be included about bisexuality, which has been defined as follows:

> The bisexual person has traditionally been stigmatized as homosexual, since specialists as well as society at large overlook the heterosexual component in favor of penalizing the homosexual component. As in the case of homosexuality, bisexuality can be defined either mentalistically or behaviorally. The most workable definition is that a bisexual person is one with a history of performing sexually with a person of either genital sex, separately or in a threesome or group.[2]

Bisexuals often meet someone of the same or opposite sex and fall in love even though they are active sexually with both sexes. In most instances they prefer sexual activity with one sex over activity with the other.

Bisexuality is often practiced by people with same-sex preferences who marry. They may have sex to satisfy their spouses and yet concurrently maintain sexual relationships or practices with members of the same sex. I have encountered a number of marriages among Christians that have broken up because one of the partners could not continue in this pattern. I have worked with men who loved their wives while at the same time enjoying sex with men they did not respect. I consider this an obsession with pleasure. A good relationship with the spouse may help to deal with the obsession, while a poor one may feed it.

In each case we have considered, the role of the person's thoughts is central. This is consistent with the biblical idea, "As he thinks within himself [literally, reckons in his soul], so he is" (Prov 23:7 marg.). This statement leads us to wonder, How do people become so different in their sexual preferences?

Causes of Same-Sex Preference

The cause of same-sex preference has been a battleground in both Christian and secular literature for a number of years. It is a hot topic because so little is known about the causes of homosexuality and because the answers put forth always have personal, political and social implications.

Historically, homosexuality has been seen as a heinous sin, a terrible sickness, a reaction to inadequate family relationships, a fluke of nature, a learned behavior or a socially acceptable alternative lifestyle. Attempts to understand homosexuality have been clouded by emotionalism and distorted by misinterpretations of what scientific evidence we have. Political entities such as the gay rights movement have a vested interest in viewing homosexuality as an irreversible, inborn condition. The following evaluation by Money and Wiedeking is as objective and up to date as any I have read:

> There is a good possibility based on experimental animal studies, that *an anomaly in prenatal hormonal function may influence sexual pathways in the central nervous system to remain sexually undifferentiated or potentially bisexual.* In human beings, an individual so affected would be vulnerable, or easily responsive to additional postnatal influences, primarily social influences that enter the brain through the eyes, ears, and skin senses, that might favor perpetuation of bipotentiality or its resolution in a homosexual differentiation of gender identity/role. Once, differentiated, a strongly homosexual gender identity/role tends to persist without changing.[3]

I have emphasized the key phrase in this explanation: a prenatal condition may predispose a person to same-sex preference. This does not mean that all persons so predisposed become homosexual, only that they may be more likely to learn same-sex preference than those who had a normal prenatal hormonal environment. Postnatal role-differentiation will determine the final outcome.

The key question, which I do not believe has been subjected to adequate investigation, is this: Can a person who has developed a homosexual identity change? The difficulties in exploring this question scientifically are obvious. We can only assume what happened prenatally, and even people with a same-sex preference are difficult to locate or unwilling to subject themselves to scientific study in such a delicate area. Psychologists are divided as to whether we should try to help a person change even if he or she asks for help. Dr. Gerald Davison, in the *Journal of Homosexuality,* writes:

> Even if one were to demonstrate that a particular sexual preference could indeed be wiped out by a negative learning experience, there remains the question as to how relevant this kind of data is to the ethical question of whether one should engage in such behavior change regimens. In discussing this possibility with some students and colleagues, I was convinced that data on efficacy are quite irrelevant. Even if we could effect certain changes, there is still the more important question of whether we should. I believe we should not.[4]

In this article Davison is speaking specifically of aversive, punishment-oriented approaches to change. In subsequent statements he and others have taken the position that any therapy provided for homosexuals should be oriented toward adjustment in their current sexual orientation and not toward change. Many Christian therapists, myself included, consider this an inadequate resolution to the problem. Pattison and Pattison, writing in the *American Journal of Psychiatry,* conclude:

> The data provide a substantial body of evidence for the plausibility of change from exclusive homosexuality to exclusive heterosexuality, which is in accordance with the Kinsey statistical probabilities for such change, the Masters and Johnson

data, and the clinical or observational anecdotes of such change. Our data demonstrate that such change has occurred through significant longitudinal experiences in "folk therapy" provided with a supernatural framework and utilizing generic methods of change common to folk therapy. Our data suggest the importance of ideology, expectation, and behavioral experience in producing change. The evidence suggests that cognitive change occurs first, followed by behavioral change, and finally intrapsychic resolution. Finally, the data suggest the importance of our concepts of homosexuality. When homosexuality is defined as an immutable and fixed condition that must be accepted, the potential for change seems slim. In our study, however, when homosexuality was defined as a changeable condition, it appears that change was possible.[5]

We need to do much more research into the religious, psychological and sociological potential for change-oriented treatment before we make any final decision. In my work I have discovered a number of people who believe themselves to be homosexuals and who have practiced homosexuality, yet who may not have been hormonally predisposed to same-sex preference in the way Money and Wiedeking have described. I say this because such people are able to relearn sexual preference rather quickly. Their filters can soon be changed, and they find themselves quite open to members of the opposite sex. The gay rights people would argue that people who change easily could not have been truly homosexual in the first place. Trying to argue that point is futile. All I am saying is that it may be counterproductive not to challenge the filters and give a person a chance to change.

I assume, based on learning theory, that people *can* change regardless of the cause of their sexual preference. When I say that homosexuality is a learned behavior, I mean that early sexual experiences unfold in such a way as to cause the person to develop same-sex preference. I believe that whereas some may be hormonally predisposed to same-sex preference, others may have learned same-sex preference without any hormonal involvement It is difficult to prove or disprove the prenatal hormonal influence theories because once same-sex preference is established, it is too late to conduct tests. In addition, women are unwilling to have their fetuses studied in utero, especially if the study is just for research purposes. Thus we are left with inference from animal studies and a few cases where medical records have shown hormone imbalance.

Most scientists are well aware that the research does not support the dogmatic pronouncements of newspaper headlines. For example, a headline in the Portland *Oregonian* read, "Homosexuals born: Indiana study finds." The research, however, was based on self-reports during five-hour interviews. Such procedures are highly questionable ways to reach sound scientific conclusions. Dr. Alan Bell, senior author of the study, indicated that the results can only be taken as theory.[6] Unfortunately the newspaper reported them as facts.

In fact, we do not have all the answers. We may not even be asking the right questions. We cannot afford to rely only on inference or opinion without continuing our research. To say change is impossible before the evidence is in may be like declaring that you won't pass a test before you even begin to study.

A Learning-Theory Analysis of Homosexuality
Previous learning theories of homosexuality have focused on the parent-child environment, assuming that family relationships affected sexual preference. My theory, based on my interaction with clients, does not deny these influences, but rather ignores them in favor of looking more carefully at actual sexual experience. In other words, my approach is that people learn sexual preference by what they observe about sex and by the type of experiences they have. I focus on what the person learns vicariously by observing parents and other adults during his or her formative years and directly during preadolescence and adolescence. I will first describe the theory and then illustrate it by telling more about Brian, the young man who decided that resisting his homosexual desires was futile.

Let us assume, as the Indiana study claimed, that ten per cent of the population has a hormonal predisposition toward same-sex preference while ninety per cent does not. Both groups are affected by early vicarious and direct learning about sex. Because of this, most people become heterosexuals, very likely including some who start with a hormonal predisposition toward same-sex preference. It is also highly probable that some of the ninety per cent will become homosexuals. In other words, those who perceive themselves as "maybe homosexual" are a mixed group, some with a hormonal predisposition to homosexuality and some without it. If we believe Masters and Johnson's conclusion that two out of three can unlearn sexual preference and Money and Wiedeking's statement that unlearning is almost impossible for the predisposed group, then we might expect about two-thirds of the people who perceive themselves as homosexuals to be able to change.

We need to backtrack to see how this works. Children are constantly learning not only sex roles but also sexual behavior from watching their parents. I first learned by watching my dad and mom that the relationship between a man and a woman could be pleasant and exciting. This made me anticipate gratifying experiences with the opposite sex in my early encounters with girls. Even though I deferred explicit sexual experience other than petting until marriage, and even though I often felt like a klutz around women, I had enough positive experiences to confirm my identity as a heterosexual.

Once early learning has established expectations, the next critical phase concerns self-perception. We develop perceptual filters which cause us to perceive and interpret input from the environment in a specific way. If my perceptual filter says, "I am a homosexual," I will tend to interpret everything that happens from that framework. If my filter says, "I am heterosexual," I will interpret data from that point of view. For example, if my filter says, "I am heterosexual," I will interpret an obscene telephone call from a male as coincidence or humorous. If my filter says, "I am a homosexual," I may take it seriously or even wonder what I did to elicit it. In other words, the filter creates an influential learning pattern.

The development of filters leads to the acceptance of a sexual identity. If I believe I am a homosexual, I am likely to become one. I begin to practice my same-sex preference, and this in turn strengthens my filter system and my acceptance of the identity. In like manner if I believe I am heterosexual, I will probably become one. In practicing my opposite-sex preference, I strengthen my filter system and accept my heterosexual identity.

Brian, who I mentioned earlier, and his sexual history illustrate my theory of sexual-identity development. Brian's early vicarious learning about sex was that a man cannot give pleasure to or receive pleasure from a woman. He had two main recollections of his parents' relationship: their fighting and the grim looks on their faces when his mother would push his father away. These memories were building blocks for his own experience.

Brian's direct sexual experience began at age thirteen. He remembers trying to make love to a neighbor girl in an abandoned house. She was stronger than he and pushed him away. He remembers feeling totally defeated. He wondered about his masculinity at that point, but didn't worry much.

When Brian entered high school, however, he became aware that he was sexually aroused by males, especially in his physical education classes. An only child, he was not used to nudity and loose sexual talk. When he occasionally found himself aroused, he didn't know what to think about it. So he responded by withdrawing as much as possible.

When Brian was seventeen he had his first homosexual encounter. He was asked to perform fellatio for a neighbor man. Because of his strong desire to please, he said yes. Even though the process made him physically ill, his strongest memory is of the man smiling and writhing in pleasure. This memory stands in sharp contrast to what he saw in his parents' relationship and what he experienced at age thirteen with the neighbor girl.

Brian became quite curious after this encounter, and the next time he was propositioned by a male he accepted. This time he didn't vomit, and he both gave and received pleasure. This experience confirmed his early perception of himself as a homosexual, and he began to develop filters to support his experience. Each new homosexual encounter strengthened his filtering system, and Brian began to develop an identity as a homosexual.

Because Brian was a believer he chose not to continue practicing homosexuality. During his college days he tried to go straight. He dated a few girls and even became engaged, but his filtering mechanism remained intact. He did not try to make love or engage in any form of sexual activity with his fiancée, eventually breaking off the engagement because of fear of not being able to satisfy her sexually.

A few years later he began to practice homosexuality on a regular basis. He truly believed his only other option was to remain sexually dormant, an option he chose not to exercise. After being in therapy a while, he began to relearn his sexual identity and reorient himself to the opposite sex. His same-sex sexual differentiation, although strong, was not permanent.

Brian's case is not sufficient to prove that same-sex preference is learned. It merely illustrates that same-sex preference can be explained from a learning point of view and that sexual preference can sometimes be relearned. We need to be careful in drawing any all-inclusive conclusions about sexual preference. I do not agree with the contention of the gay rights movement that homosexuals are born that way and therefore cannot change. An individual who accepts this position may be selling his birthright to natural heterosexual experience. On the other hand, I do not believe that we can say that all homosexuals without question can relearn their sexual orientation. We need to continue to do careful research to determine the characteristics of those who change and those who do not.

From a Christian perspective my concern is that the issue not become a battle between the haves and the have-nots, the spiritual who change and the nonspiritual who do not. We are talking about people God loves. I have counseled some Christians who, believing they cannot change, have chosen a life of celibacy as their way of being obedient to God. They have my deepest respect. We dare not develop a caste system based on homosexual and heterosexual lust. Lust is lust, and Scripture challenges us not to be controlled by it in any form. My hat is off to any person regardless of sexual preference who honestly faces the matter and struggles to honor God by the choices he or she makes.

Homosexual Obsession

In the final analysis homosexuality must be treated like any other type of sexual obsession. The first-hand account of a person struggling with homosexual temptation shows the extent of the struggle. Bill describes a typical scene:

> I was sitting in a coffee shop, drinking tea and thumbing through a newspaper, when I noticed a good-looking man at a table across the room. I watched him and realized (with a thrill of excitement) that I'd seen him there before. We hadn't met, but I knew I had been wildly attracted to him then, and I had sensed he was interested in me. Somehow, I don't know how, I knew he was gay.
>
> I then noticed him looking at me, then back at his writing, then back at me again, several times. My thoughts raced. "He remembers me," I thought, "and he wouldn't be paying me this kind of attention unless he wanted to make love to me." I hoped he would come over to my table, and I kept looking in his direction. All this time, of course, my internal alarm bells were ringing. I knew I was playing with fire, but I stayed there, feeling aroused and ashamed of myself at the same time, flattered by his attention but afraid to make eye contact with him, and conscious above all else of a tingling, surging sensation flowing through me like an electrical current. This went on for fifteen or twenty minutes, until he got up and left the shop. By this time my conscience had regained control and the floods of excitement were receding, but even then temptation got the better of me. I followed him at a distance but lost him, still thinking about making love with him, *disappointed but relieved.*

Bill's final words reveal the extent of the battle against obsession. Bill was both disappointed and relieved.

Shortly after this temptation Bill made the hard decision to attack his sexual obsessions directly. He summarized his decision in a letter to Greg, a former lover.

As I share Bill's letter with you, which he graciously agreed to allow me to print here, I pray for spiritual victory for him and for all those caught in homosexual obsessions.

Dear Greg,

After we talked the other night, you were probably left with the impression that I'm keeping you at arm's length. I can see it's time to level with you, and I apologize for not having done so earlier.

I have to tell you that I don't want any further contact between us, because I don't want to resume the physical relationship we had before.

Following the breakup of my first gay relationship three years ago, I became a Christian, and I've come to believe that all homosexual acts are wrong, in and of themselves. Although I'm still attracted to other men, I believe there is at least a possibility of change in my sexual orientation, and I'm currently undergoing professional counseling.

In any case, however, I've chosen not to live a gay lifestyle and—God helping me—I'm doing my best not to compromise. For me, there is great danger in becoming emotionally involved with a man to whom I'm already attracted sexually. I don't want anything more to come of this relationship, and so I believe it's best to leave well enough alone.

Good-by, Greg. I wish you well.

Bill

It is vital that the church stand behind people like Bill who want to follow Jesus Christ and are striving to please him. Homosexuals are not people to be feared. Most of them are sensitive people who need God's redemptive healing just as you and I do.

Part III
Returning to
Sexual Sanity

8
Facing Temptation

TODAY'S SOCIETY IS SO PERMEATED with enticements to sex that even the most innocent Christian is affected. If you do not experience sexual temptation directly, you can still see its effects in the lives of those close to you. Christians face the ever-growing challenge of responsibility in a world characterized by sexual irresponsibility. As the prophet asked, "How should we then live?" (Ezek 33:10 KJV).

The reality of sexual temptation presents several specific challenges for the serious Christian. How should I react to a sexually explicit society? What standards will I seek to live by? How can I accept sex as a gift from God and at the same time avoid the pressure to exploit the gift? What attitude should I take when I fail? What do I do about recurring sexual sin? Are some ways of dealing with temptation wrong or unproductive? Does God know what I'm facing? Does he care?

These and many other questions rush into the minds of believers with all too regular frequency. In this chapter I will try to give practical suggestions which will better equip you to face the sinful world in which we live. The last questions were the most important. I will address them first.

Does God Know? Does He Care?

The Bible answers these questions with an emphatic yes! Scripture is clear that Jesus, our Savior and High Priest, was tempted himself and understands our temptation. Take comfort from Hebrews 4:14-16:

> Therefore, since we have a great high priest who has gone through the heavens, Jesus the Son of God, let us hold firmly to the faith we profess. For we do not have a high priest who is unable to sympathize with our weaknesses, but we have one who has been tempted in every way, just as we are—yet was without sin. Let us then approach the throne of grace with confidence, so that we may receive mercy and find grace to help us in our time of need.

In recognizing the temptation that Peter was going to experience, Jesus showed how much he cared: "Simon, Simon, Satan has asked to sift you as wheat. But I have prayed for you, Simon, that your faith may not fail. And when you have turned back, strengthen your brothers" (Lk 22:31-32).

It is certain that God knows our struggles, understands and forgives our failures but longs for our success. The question most people face when confronted with temptation is not "Does God care?" but "Do I care?" I usually find that he has made more resources available to me that I am willing to employ. I sin because I choose to sin rather than because I am left without resources by a God who doesn't care.

As a teen-ager I memorized 1 Corinthians 10:13. Over the past thirty years I have found it to be true and helpful every time I have applied it to a temptation I was facing. According to the apostle

Paul, "no temptation has seized you except what is common to man. And God is faithful; he will not let you be tempted beyond what you can bear. But when you are tempted, he will also provide a way out so that you can stand up under it." Whenever I have ignored the resources offered to me by God, however, I have failed.

How Should I Respond to a Sexually Explicit Society?

An often quoted bit of folk wisdom says, "If you can't beat 'em, join 'em." When you compare the lifestyle of many Christians with that of nonbelievers, it appears that that, in fact, is what has happened. It is sometimes hard to discern any difference in the two lifestyles. Christians have not always made good decisions about relating to our sexually saturated society. But rather than wasting time berating ourselves for past failures, we need to encourage one another in this important area. Let us consider our options.

Many believers think that the best option is to *ignore* the world and its temptations. Act like it doesn't exist. After I spoke to a youth rally in Kansas, a parent told me that I shouldn't have talked about sex. He said, "If you talk about it, some of those kids are going to go out and get pregnant." He seemed completely unaware of the extent to which young people's lives are already affected by our sex-soaked society. I told him we could try to ignore sex, but it wasn't likely to go away.

I was asked to give a series of lectures on pornography to young adults at my own church. After the first talk I was confronted by a young woman and her father who felt strongly that I should not have spoken so openly about the types of sin available out there. They believed that by making people aware you may encourage them to participate. I listened, tried to take them seriously and studied carefully the text they used to support their view. Together we read:

The night is nearly over; the day is almost here. So let us put aside the deeds of darkness and put on the armor of light. Let us behave decently, as in the daytime, not in orgies and drunkenness, not in sexual immorality and debauchery, not in dissension and jealousy. Rather, clothe yourselves with the Lord

Jesus Christ, and do not think about how to gratify the desires of the sinful nature. (Rom 13:12-14)

I respect their position, but I still believe that we must know the enemy and understand both the subtle and the obvious ways he tries to affect us. Making people aware of dangers is not the same as thinking about how to gratify the desires of the sinful nature.

Other believers hold that we must respond to the world by *fighting* sin in any form, with force if necessary (see Ezek 3:19). There is a place for becoming politically involved in the fight against pornography, prostitution, sexual abuse of children, and other sexual sins that affect society. The Holy Spirit works through believers to restrain evil. We need to be careful that laws designed to protect individual freedom are not used to protect the rights of only a few while violating the rights of the masses to be protected against people whose aberrations endanger society. Although I am sensitive to this fight, I have chosen to concentrate on helping individuals who are struggling against sexual problems in a personal way. We must fight at both levels, but we must not lose sight of the fact that sexual sin always has been and always will be around. We must be alert to its effects upon us personally and as a society.

No Christian should ignore the world, and not all Christians are called to fight against society's evils. But all Christians are called to do two things: resist temptation and penetrate society as salt and light.

Believers are commanded to *resist* the evil that in in the world. James 4:7 sets the pattern for this type of action: "Submit yourselves, then, to God. Resist the devil, and he will flee from you." What does it mean to resist sexual temptation? I believe that to resist is to choose—to choose not to become involved. I have worked with many people who were involved in sexual sins, not intentionally, but because they did not choose *not* to get involved. When I am tempted by the sight of a voluptuous woman I have a choice to make. I can choose to continue the pattern of thoughts that the visual stimulus has triggered, or I can choose to control my thinking and move on to other things. I might say to myself, "That was interesting, but I choose not to pursue it." Remembering Philippians 4:8 can be a real help at this point: "Finally, brothers, whatever is true, whatever is noble, whatever is right, whatever is pure, whatever is lovely, whatever is admirable—if anything is excellent or praiseworthy—think about such things."

Resisting also involves taking action to get out of harm's way. Notice Solomon's advice: "Now then, my sons, listen to me; pay attention to what I say. Do not let your heart turn to her ways or stray into her paths. Many are the victims she has brought down; her slain are a mighty throng. Her house is a highway to the grave, leading down to the chambers of death" (Prov 7:24-27). This passage contains three specific and helpful bits of advice for a person who wants to resist temptation. First, pay attention to God's Word. Don't let your desire for sexual satisfaction cause you to go against truth or common sense. Obsessional thinking is usually permeated with poor judgment and failure to adequately assess the situation. Some people become so blind that they fail to realize their behavior is a violation not only of biblical standards but also of civil law. One man said, "I just never thought about the fact that I could go to prison."

Second, the passage says, "Don't let your heart turn to her ways." Sound thinking based on God's Word must be followed by taking charge of your emotions. You can choose not to be controlled by troublesome feelings.

The obsessional thought says, "You can't live without stimulation." Your emotions will try to pull you in that direction. Solomon says, "Don't turn your heart." One way to resist something is to put your thoughts, emotions and energies into behavior that is incompatible with the temptation. Jesus used this method to overcome suffering. In 1 Peter 2:23 we read: "When they hurled their insults at him, he did not retaliate; when he suffered, he made no threats. Instead, he entrusted himself to him who judges justly." The words I want to emphasize are "entrusted himself." This could be translated, "kept on entrusting himself." Even Jesus had to repeatedly make the hard choice of putting himself in God's care rather than walking in the way of temptation.

Third, resisting temptation requires control of behavior. Just thinking the right thoughts and controlling my emotions is not enough. I need to be in charge of my actions as well. The verse says, "Do not stray." I must deliberately choose to walk away from, not toward, temptation. My ability to make this choice of action will come from my proper thoughts and my controlled emotions. God prepares the escape route or the resistance plan, but I must choose to use it.

As important as personal resistance to temptation is, Christians have a responsibility that goes beyond themselves. Believers are also called to be salt and light in our sexually explicit society. In the Sermon on the Mount, Jesus used salt and light as analogies for our behavior. In Matthew 5:13-16 we read:

> You are the salt of the earth. But if the salt loses its saltiness, how can it be made salty again? It is no longer good for anything, except to be thrown out and trampled by men. You are the light of the world. A city on a hill cannot be hidden. Neither do people light a lamp and put it under a bowl. Instead they put it on its stand, and it gives light to everyone in the house. In the same way, let your light shine before men, that they may see your good deeds and praise your Father in heaven.

How do these verses apply to sexual temptation?

Salt has two main functions, seasoning and preservation. Much sex in today's world is flat, like tasteless food. As mentioned earlier, promiscuity often results in sex without pleasure, and pornography leads to boredom. But God gave scriptural rules and guidelines to enable us to enjoy salty sex for a lifetime. We need to resist temptation not by resisting sex, but by showing that within the boundaries set by God sex has a full, zesty flavor. Christians should be the sexiest people in the world, because we know that God made us capable of enjoying full, lasting sex within marriage.

Salt is also a preservative. We need to preserve God's design for sexual fulfillment. The world is full of sexual experiments and crazy schemes. Our role is to maintain high-quality sex within marriage as the standard by which all experiments may be judged. Even in our sin-crushed society, this role is working. Individuals (not the masses) are realizing that living for sexual pleasure does not bring lasting satisfaction. Not even pleasure can be preserved without the salt of Christian truth.

Jesus also spoke of Christians as light. Light is expressive and active, not passive. It reaches out to people and demands a response. We cannot hide the light under a bushel. We need to let it shine. If Christian values regarding sex are worth holding, they are worth projecting.

The person who lives in a restored relationship with God and is indwelt by the Holy Spirit is in a unique position to respond to sexual temptation in God's strength rather than in human weakness. We need to stay clear of the pitfalls of sexual temptation so that we let the light shine on a better way. This is a tremendous challenge in the modern world and a great goal.

What Do I Do When I Fail?

It is easy to maintain our perspective when we are successfully resisting sexual temptation, but it is hard to keep our priorities in order when we have given in. "What's the use?" we are likely to think. "I blew it, so I might as well do the other things I have been tempted to do." This attitude, which leads to deep guilt and spiritual as well as sexual frustration, is not the approach recommended by Jesus. When Jesus confronted individuals who had sinned and who were repentant, his response was always the same. He forgave the sin and challenged the person to forsake it and to begin living a better way. In John 8:7-11, when Jesus is confronted by those who caught a woman in adultery, we read:

"If any one of you is without sin, let him be the first to throw a stone at her." Again he stooped down and wrote on the ground. At this, those who heard began to go away one at a time, the older ones first, until only Jesus was left, with the woman still standing there. Jesus straightened up and asked her, "Woman, where are they? Has no one condemned you?"

"No one, sir," she said.

"Then neither do I condemn you," Jesus declared. "Go now and leave your life of sin."

In his book on self-control, Paul Hauck stresses the need to take responsibility for each failure and not to let failures add up. He writes:

> If you allow yourself to taste that fleeting pleasure once, you are obviously quite tempted to do it again and again. That's why disciplining oneself is usually so hard: you are fighting against a whole series of immediate rewards that are in competition with immediate frustrations and *later* rewards. But if you keep in mind that later rewards are often more beneficial than the immediate ones, you will find it less difficult to discipline yourself.[1]

The most crucial point to deal with a recurring temptation may be immediately following a failure. At that time we can choose to let failure become a habit, or we can choose to continue to resist the temptation with renewed vigor. We will be ambivalent. We will want to resist, but we will also desire the pleasures of sin. Seeing the sin from God's perspective is crucial. Having a friend who holds us accountable may be most helpful.

To guard against guilt and defeat, it is also important to accept God's forgiveness. Many Christians who struggle with sexual temptation have experienced repeated failures that have deeply affected their relationship with God. It is hard to go back to God again and again when we are so painfully aware of our failures. Satan wants us to feel unworthy so we will not go back to God. He makes us forget that God is longsuffering and always willing to forgive. In Psalm 86:15 we read, "You, O Lord, are a compassionate and gracious God, slow to anger, abounding in love and faithfulness."

The apostle Peter presents a similar view of God's forgiving nature: "The Lord is not slow in keeping his promise, as some understand slowness. He is patient with you, not wanting anyone to perish, but everyone to come to repentance" (2 Pet 3:9).

God understands our need for repeated forgiveness. Jesus showed this when Peter asked how often to forgive. "Then Peter came to Jesus and asked, 'Lord, how many times shall I forgive my brother when he sins against me? Up to seven times?' Jesus answered, 'I tell you, not seven times, but seventy-seven times' " (Mt 18:21-22).

In Psalm 103, a song of praise for the Lord's mercies, David stresses that sin is both forgiven and removed from God's mind. "He does not treat us as our sins deserve or repay us according to our iniquities. For as high as the heavens are above the earth, so great is his love for those who fear him; as far as the east is from the west, so far has he removed our transgressions from us. As a father has compassion on his children, so the LORD has compassion on those who fear him; for he knows how we are formed, he remembers that we are dust" (Ps 103:10-14). Each time we confess a sin to God, he treats it like a new offense. He does not keep a record of our sins but stands ready to forgive even the recurring sin. Hebrews 10:17 quotes God's word to Jeremiah: "Their sins and lawless acts I will remember no more." God's marvelous capacity to completely forgive and forget is the only hope for people who are caught in patterns of recurring sin.

Many Christians want to believe this, but they have trouble doing so because they hope that once forgiven they will not repeat the sin. I too would like to be released from habitual sin, but I know that often when I try the hardest I fail. As a believer I am responsible to continually bring my sin to God, whether it is a repeated sin or not. From my perspective it may be a cancer and a sign of failure. From his perspective it is a new sin, and he longs to forgive. If, however, I spend all my time loathing my habit, I am doing nothing more than insuring that it will continue. I need to focus on Christ, not sin.

Once I have admitted the sinfulness of my sin—that is, once I see sin as God sees it, and am led to repentance—I need to keep my attention focused on my Savior and not on my sin. Continuing to mentally replay my sin can itself be an obsession. God wants to talk to me. He wants to have fellowship with me.

How would you feel if you wanted to talk with friends or family and all they would talk about was how badly they had hurt you? This would be particularly disturbing if you had already forgiven them and had told them so not once but many times. God has already forgiven us. His Son, Jesus, has paid all our debts. We may cry because we are penniless and in debt, but God knows that Jesus has filled our accounts. We are forgiven!

From a strictly psychological point of view, the worst thing we can do if we want to stop a habit is to focus on it. Even trying to stop thinking about something will make us think of it more.

If you are thinking about stopping an undesirable habit, recycle your thoughts. Don't waste time thinking about how not to think about it. This will only draw you into quicksand. Instead, keep your thoughts in good places. Focus on Christ and the good things he has done and is doing in your life.

Not long ago I was so hungry I thought I would surely die if I didn't eat in the next thirty-seven seconds. I left the hotel where I was attending a meeting, hoping to find a good restaurant before I passed out. Just then I saw a motorcade coming up the street, and I became involved in the excitement. Rumor was that it might be accompanying Senator Mark Hatfield. I admire him so much that I turned and followed the cars, hoping to see who was inside. Twenty minutes later I was still working my way through the crowd. I stopped at a crosswalk and as I looked across the intersection I saw a restaurant. I was glad, but an amazing thing had happened. I wasn't hungry anymore. When my attention was focused on the hope of seeing Senator Hatfield, my obsession with food was diminished.

I believe this is the only way recurring sin will be conquered. Notice the way that Hebrews 12:1-3 addresses the issue:

Let us throw off everything that hinders and the sin that so easily entangles, and let us run with perseverance the race marked out for us. Let us fix our eyes on Jesus, the author and perfecter of our faith, who for the joy set before him endured the cross, scorning its shame, and sat down at the right hand of the throne of God. Consider him who endured such opposition from sinful men, so that you will not grow weary and lose heart.

When we fix our eyes on Jesus, we see victory. This gives us hope. When we fix our eyes on our recurring sin, we will see only defeat and will become ashamed to look at Jesus. We don't need that kind of hopelessness. We need to get our attention back on the source of hope. This is why a regular time of reading Scripture and praying is so helpful. It puts our attention on Christ where it belongs.

Rock climbing is a challenging sport. If done properly it involves careful teamwork. The climber's life is literally in the hands of the person who controls the safety rope. When I climb, I may stumble, slip and even fall. I could become discouraged or frightened by looking at the sharp cliff above or the drop below. But I can maintain nervous and mental stability by fixing my mind on the fact that the person on the other end of that rope is not going to let me fall. When I know my partner is committed to my safety, I can try new things and learn new ways to get up or down the cliff. If I trust, I will not find myself hanging by my fingertips expecting to fall at any moment.

I must say it again—look at the Savior, not at the sin.

How Not to Avoid Temptation
I know many people with great hearts for God and yet great feelings of failure because of recurring sexual sins. In the process of sharing in their lives, I have discovered several ways they have tried to deal with temptation which for one reason or another did not work.

One ill-fated method is to try to make yourself undesirable. Putting on layers of fat or layers of grouchiness are common examples. A woman told me, "I knew I wasn't strong enough to resist sex because my needs are so great, so I thought I could avoid the problem by getting so fat no one would ever want to have sex with me." A young man said, "As long as I was rude and mean I thought I would avoid the trouble. I didn't want to cause other people to stumble, so I tried to scare them away."

My heart went out to both these people. They were so sincere and yet so miserable. I pointed out that God's will is not accomplished by destroying his creation—you. The power to resist temptation comes with wholeness, not brokenness or destruction. There has to be a better way.

Most who try to handle temptation this way often increase their needs and are thus tempted to sin through private fantasies. Putting on fat or grouchiness is no substitute for putting on the whole armor of God (Eph 6:10-18). When struggling with sexual temptation, we need to be able to accept ourselves—our own personality and body. We should thank God for the positive attributes he has given us, taking good care of them and asking him to help us resist temptation without destroying his handiwork. God does not want to see us destroyed but fulfilled sexually in accordance with his plan.

A second ineffective way of dealing with sexual temptation is to try to get it all out of our system. The human capacity for sexual sin is insatiable. We are only kidding ourselves if we think we can try it just once and then we won't want it anymore. This is Satan's trap. Taking a bite out of the apple will only increase our guilt and make us more vulnerable. Those who have tried it usually feel weaker, not stronger.

Another misguided method is to deny your sexuality. Many people have tried so hard to please God that they have lost touch with who they are. One person said, "I don't have any feelings anymore. I just won't let myself feel anything."

The main problem with repression is that it doesn't work. Phillip Swihart writes:

Repression comes at great cost for it saps our energies like a hidden short in an electrical system. It takes effort to keep these feelings hidden in the recesses of our unconscious. As a child, did you ever play with a bit of wood or a balloon, trying to push it under the surface of a tank of water? It was fun and fascinating because it was so difficult to keep it from floating to the surface. Keeping down feelings that we fear will blow up in our face or reveal us as some kind of monster is an energy drain that leaves us less able to help others and to be about the King's business in general.[2]

Acknowledging your sexual desires and asking God to show you how to channel them is much better than acting as if they don't exist. When you ignore them they usually don't go away. They pop up in other ways, and people often give in because they feel unable to keep the block of wood under the water. It is much more effective to let the wood float but at the same time to control the drift. Floating material is easier to guide than to submerge.

A Better Way

Any discussion of sexual temptation would be incomplete without a look at the way David dealt with his sin and looked for a new attitude. David was honest with God, which may be why, despite his sin, he was called a man after God's own heart. May you take comfort and find guidance from his honest expression of his experience. In Psalm 51:5-12 he writes:

Surely I have been a sinner from birth, sinful from the time my mother conceived me. Surely you desire truth in the inner parts; you teach me wisdom in the inmost place. Cleanse me with hyssop, and I will be clean; wash me, and I will be whiter than snow. Let me hear joy and gladness; let the bones you have crushed rejoice. Hide your face from my sins and blot out all my iniquity. Create in me a pure heart, O God, and renew a steadfast spirit within me. Do not cast me from your presence or take your Holy Spirit from me. Restore to me the joy of your salvation and grant me a willing spirit, to sustain me.

God is good!

9
Overcoming Sexual Obsession

SANDY, MY WIFE, AND I HAD JUST settled down to watch the late evening news when the telephone rang. Reluctantly, I got up to answer it. In my mind I said telephone calls after 11:00 P.M. are not usually good. I was right. Tom, one of my clients was calling, and he was very upset. "It won't stop," he said, "as hard as I am trying, I can't make the thoughts stop."

Tom was downtown and had called in desperation because he was about to make the rounds of the adult bookstores. "I don't want to do that again," he said. "I don't want the guilt but I just can't seem to get the thoughts out of my head."

I knew Tom well and I knew the hell he was going through. Even though he had made progress his resources at this moment seemed so limited. As we talked Tom began to regain control. I rehearsed with him several steps which he could use to overcome the terrible pull he was feeling.

Accepting God's Forgiveness

Because sexual obsession is sin we must deal with it as with any other sin. Most believers are well aware intellectually that God forgives us for all of our sins, including sexual sins. However, because of the pleasures associated with sexual obsessions, we often delay dealing with them as sin and continue indulging them. This results in increased guilt and decreased personal integrity.

Mary, age twenty-seven, lived with obsessive sexual thoughts for ten years. Early in her college experience she discovered her strong sexual desire and began to indulge it both mentally and physically. She carefully protected her virginity in the technical sense, but became increasingly sexually active.

Her thinking grew more and more legalistic until she labeled sexual intercourse as sin but denied the sinfulness of heavy petting. Although she was obsessed with sex, she came to believe her body was ugly and evil. For a long time she refused to acknowledge sin, and when she finally did, she refused to confess it because she felt hypocritical. She was caught in a trap, unable either to receive God's forgiveness or to enjoy her sexuality as a gift from God. Her mental health hung by a thread.

After several sessions with a counselor and much patient support and wise guidance from a pastor, she was able to experience what David describes in Psalm 32:5: "I acknowledged my sin to you and did not cover up my iniquity. I said, 'I will confess my transgressions to the LORD'—and you forgave the guilt of my sin." Have you ever thought how it must grieve God, since he knows that Christ died to provide forgiveness from sin, to see people go to the brink of suicide rather than receive the free gift? There can be no deliverance from any sin without seeking and receiving God's gift of forgiveness.

Sanctification Is a Process

Ted was twenty-eight-years old when I first met him. Referred to me by a crisis hot line, he reluctantly agreed to come in and talk. Ted was a believer but now felt miserable and suicidal. I learned that he was a practicing homosexual before his conversion and had been told that when he received Christ he would be delivered from his sinful habit. That was three years ago.

Sitting in my office, he cried out in anguish as he told of his continuing struggle with homosexual desire. Neither scriptural instruction nor human logic could convince him that his lack of deliverance was not proof of God's rejection and lack of love for him. He could not accept his own continued failure, and he could not understand a God who refused to deliver him as his spiritual fathers had promised.

One week later Ted drove his car into the bay.

Even though I barely knew this young man, I realized that a valuable life had been wasted. "Why?" I asked myself. Two answers emerged. First, his spiritual mentors had not been straight with him. Deliverance from sin is often a process, not an immediate product of regeneration as they had told Ted. Deliverance depends on obedience and is rarely experienced as a quick cure.

Second, no one had helped Ted prepare for the failures encountered on the way to victory. The help I tried to give him was too little too late. God forgives us our sin each time we confess it. He longs to see his healing power at work on our obsessive sins. The key is to persevere, realizing that God is faithful and that forgiveness is effective, even when change is not permanent. If your obsession is strong, you might need to confess your sin and receive forgiveness a hundred times a day. But it is not futile. It is a process.

Stopping Thoughts

My wife, Sandy, and I were deeply engaged in a conversation one evening when we heard a terrible bang upstairs. We both rushed up to find our son crawling back up to the top bunk. After seeing that he was all right we returned to the coffee table and supposedly to our conversation. There was only one problem—neither of us could remember what we had been talking about. Our thoughts had been stopped by the sudden interruption.

Stopping thoughts can be a powerful tool in battling sexual obsessions. When you find yourself lapsing into a destructive thought pattern, slap yourself on the leg and say, "Stop!" Then move on to a productive thought.

Bill had been arrested for fondling his daughter and was referred to my colleague for counseling. Touching the child was truly an obsession for him. The counselor helped Bill identify the chain of events that he went through in the process of going to the child's bed. Bill, who wanted to change, agreed to stop his obsessive thoughts as soon as they occurred so that he would not continue the undesirable behavior. Bill practiced the technique in the counselor's office. The counselor told him to use it when the child came home for a trial visit.

At his next appointment, Bill reported partial success. The counselor then asked him to recreate the situation by verbalizing his thoughts and role-playing his actions. When Bill came to the crucial thoughts, he said "Stop" in a whisper and went right ahead with the undesired behavior.

The counselor said, "Let's go through that again." Bill began to whisper, and the counselor shouted, "Stop!" This brought different results. Bill could hardly remember what he had done next, even though he was role-playing a real situation. The next time the child visited he was prepared to stop his thoughts, even if he had to shout. This time he succeeded.

Another useful technique is using a rubber band worn loosely around your wrist. Each time the undesirable thought occurs, give yourself a flip and say, "Stop." The slight punishment coupled with the thought interruption will serve to sidetrack, at least temporarily, the undesired thinking.

Obsessive thoughts can usually be identified by their frequency or intensity. *I must* or *I should* are common cues. *Catastrophizing* or *glamorizing* are also common. "If I can't see these pictures it will be awful" is an example of catastrophizing. Choosing to savor the forbidden is glamorizing—thinking only of potential pleasure without either evaluating the activity from a moral standpoint or asking yourself if acting on the fantasy is what you really want.

When undesirable thoughts occur, often they can be controlled by stopping them as soon as possible and focusing on other things as long as possible. Scripture meditation and prayer can be invaluable aids in this process. Building scriptural principles into your thoughts and emotions provides a basis for a strong positive thought life.

The brain cannot stay in neutral for long. Stopping the thought is not enough; you must redirect it!

Not Being a Squeegee

In *The Undivided Self* I suggest that we tend to react to responsibility as if it were a puddle in the middle of the floor—we attack it with either a squeegee or a sponge. Sometimes we immediately squeegee the blame onto the nearest person with little or no regard for the facts of the situation. This defense mechanism, unfortunately, is widely used.

Vern was first referred to me by his roommates, who were concerned about his lifestyle. Recently Vern had developed a pattern of staying out late and being gone from the apartment for long periods of time. He also seemed to grow secretive and emotionally distant. He came for counseling even though he was skeptical about the outcome because he was unwilling to hurt his roommates' feelings.

Vern did not want his roommates to know that he had begun to indulge some of his sexual fantasies. He was beginning to tell himself, "God made me this way! I can't change! I can't control myself! Therefore, I have to live out my lustful thoughts." He was laying the blame at God's feet rather than taking responsibility for his own behavior.

Were Vern's basic assumptions correct? We examined them one by one. "God made me this way." There is no question that God invented human sexuality. He gave sexual desire to men and women for their pleasure and for the propagation and preservation of the human race. Human sexual arousal, like many other good gifts, can be used correctly according to God's purpose or incorrectly by distorting this purpose. Lust is an inappropriate practice of our God-given capacity for sexual arousal. It was Vern who chose to pursue lustful pleasures outside the boundaries set by God, not God who "made him this way." Vern's developing pattern of obsessional thinking was driving him to feel he could not survive without expressing his desires. Since he believed his desires were too strong ever to be fulfilled within marriage, he thought he had no choice but to live an immoral life.

"I can't control myself." Vern seriously believed this statement because it summarized his sexual experience to date. He could not even enjoy the girls in his church youth group because he was sure he had no control over himself. Believing something, however, doesn't make it true. Vern was very controlled in other areas of his life.

I encouraged Vern to become a scientist and to test his belief. He found that when he applied the principles of self-control that worked in other areas of his life to the sexual area, they did indeed work. He also came to realize that God is faithful if we choose to trust him. Paul's promise in 1 Corinthians 10:13, "God is faithful; he will not let you be tempted beyond what you can bear. But when you are tempted, he will also provide a way out," began to take on a new meaning for him.

Sexual desire is a hard taskmaster that can control and destroy us if we choose to serve it. Choosing not to serve it is difficult, but possible. The key is accepting responsibility for our actions without blaming God or others.

We often think we can't change because we filter our experiences so they validate our beliefs about ourselves. I have come to realize that I am an expert at hearing what I want to hear so that I can believe what I want to believe so that I can do what I want to do. Obsessional thinking invariably leads to this kind of selective perception of our environment. We hear what we want to hear or see what we want to see because we are unwilling to see anything that would facilitate change or growth. Undoubtedly this is what the prophet had observed when he wrote about "people who have eyes but do not see, who have ears but do not hear" (Jer 5:21).

In trying to change undesirable behavior patterns many people make a serious mistake. They stress stopping the undesirable without giving adequate attention to building the behavior they want. In the book of Colossians, which emphasizes Christian growth, Paul affirms three necessities for change: put off, put on, let in (see Col 2—3). We need to *put off* the obsessions and *put on* higher thoughts, thoughts that go beyond physical stimulation.

> Since, then, you have been raised with Christ, set your hearts on things above, where Christ is seated at the right hand of God. Set your minds on things above, not on earthly things. For you died, and your life is now hidden with Christ in God. When Christ, who is your life, appears, then you also will appear with him in glory. Put to death, therefore, whatever belongs to your earthly nature: sexual immorality, impurity, lust, evil desires and greed, which is idolatry. (Col 3:1-5)

We also need to *let in* the truth about the sexuality God has given us. It is good. It can bring enjoyment. It doesn't have to torment us. Many people, especially men, have never learned to enjoy their sexuality at a relational level. That is, they have not learned to see members of the opposite sex as people and to enjoy relating with them without pursuing sexual intercourse as the major purpose in life. Obviously, change at this level requires opening up to God the habits of inappropriate thought. These too can be broken. But additional help is needed.

Being Accountable

I have found that Christians who try to play the Lone Ranger often get themselves into trouble. When faced with difficulty they do not have the support they need. Lone Christians also lack the guidance of others who will hold them responsible for their behavior. A support and responsibility system is particularly crucial for those who are struggling to overcome sexual obsessions.

When I talked with Jim he was frightened because he had just had a close call with the law. For a number of years he had been leaving his home at night and walking about town looking for a female he could watch undressing or making love. Jim hated the term *peeping Tom,* and yet he readily admitted that in the last few years he had become just that. This voyeuristic obsession had become so strong and he exercised his habit so frequently that it is not surprising that one night he almost ran into a policeman. After his scare he felt so guilty that he almost wished he had been caught.

As a Christian struggling with this severe problem, Jim took two risks. One was to ask to talk to me, a caring professional. The other was to tell his Christian roommate about his problem and to ask for his prayers and support. This took great courage, for Jim was well aware that he might be totally rejected.

Jim was fortunate. His roommate not only enthusiastically agreed to pray, but he also told Jim to feel free to discuss his desires and temptations any time, day or night. Jim went one step further and asked his roommate to check his progress once a week. The roommate's role was not to punish Jim if he failed, but rather to encourage him in his successes. He was to "rejoice with those who rejoice; mourn with those who mourn" (Rom 12:15).

The roommate was not a psychologist to help answer the why questions—that was my job—but rather a friend to whom Jim would be accountable. Jim reported that just knowing he would have to tell his roommate was sometimes enough to detour his activities. God also used the roommate to help Jim gain some of the self-confidence he needed.

Breaking the Chain

I have been saying that thought stopping and thought substitution are important steps in dealing with obsessional behavior. Now I want to fine-tune this idea by giving specific suggestions on how to break a chain of obsessional thinking.

A behavioral chain is simply a pattern in which one thought or behavior triggers another, which triggers another, which triggers yet another. In a chain of obsessional thinking, a rather innocent thought leads to one that is less innocent, which in turn leads to more dangerous thoughts and behavior until acting on the obsession is complete.

Susie came to see me because she was depressed and was becoming dissatisfied with her marriage. After a couple of hours of exploring her problem I discovered that she was heavily involved in sexual fantasy which was sapping her emotional energy. She was spending hours each day watching soap operas and mentally living out her sexual life through the lives of the women on the screen. As we examined her behavior pattern the following chain of thoughts and behaviors became apparent.

Susie's husband worked nights and would get home and fall into bed about the time she had to get up with the young children. A morning person, she was often sexually sensitive when she woke up. She would approach her husband but he was seldom responsive. He occasionally gave her enough attention to arouse her but not enough to satisfy her. After a while Susie gave up. She told me, "I decided I would be aroused the rest of my life."

Much to Susie's surprise she began to read love stories with her morning coffee, and then she began watching the soaps regularly. It wasn't long before she had established a new pattern. Every morning she slipped out of bed without so much as snuggling with her husband, got the children off to school and settled down for hours of uninterrupted fantasy. Her housework suffered, her relationships with friends dwindled and her husband became less and less important to her sex life. She recognized that her behavior contradicted her beliefs, but she felt trapped and unable to break out of the cycle. Susie was trying to break the habit, but she wasn't making much headway.

Together we diagrammed the chain of events that happened every morning (figure 1).

I asked Susie when she usually tried to break the chain. She answered, "When I start to feel guilty." We explored this further and discovered that she usually felt guilty three times: when the children were getting after her to make breakfast—links 9, 10, 11; when she began to stimulate herself physically—link 17; and when she began to engage in full-blown fantasy during the latter part of the morning—link 21. I asked why she didn't stop the chain

```
wake up ——▶ feel sexual tension ——▶ watch husband sleep ——▶ feel frustrated
  1                2                          3                      4        │
wake children ◀——————— make coffee ◀——————— find book ◀——————— get up ▼
     8                      7                    6                  5
│
▼ start reading ——————▶ feed children ——————▶ feel frustrated ——————▶ read more
     9                      10                    11                    12
                                                                             │
  read book ◀—— pour coffee ◀—— drive children to school ◀—— dress children ▼
     16            15                    14                        13
▼ rub body ——————▶ read more ——————▶ turn on soaps ——————▶ watch two hours
     17              18                  19                    20
                                                                    │
  fantasize about making love ◀————————————————— reluctantly fix dinner ▼
              22                                              21
```

Figure 1

when the children were nagging her. Her answer was revealing. "They didn't make me feel bad enough. I blamed my discomfort on them."

Susie was waiting too long to break the chain. Once the more stimulating or rewarding aspects of the chain have begun, not even guilt feelings are strong enough to break it. Thought substitution is difficult when undesired thoughts have been entertained until they become desirable. I encouraged Susie to attack the chain at the beginning where the links are weakest.

We talked about things she could think when she first woke up that would get her headed away from her obsessional thoughts. She could pray or read her Bible or plan her day. We also talked about experiencing her sexual feelings without catastrophizing them. She learned to say, "I'm aroused and that's okay. I'll just savor snuggling up to Bill. He won't sleep forever and he does like to have sex with me."

Susie next assaulted the chain at link 6. Having decided to make her obsession more difficult by getting rid of some of her books, she replaced reading with talking to and playing with her children as they woke up. She felt good about this decision. It reinforced her move in the right direction, and it also tended to direct some of her sexual energies.

Susie's final attack on the chain was at link 14, when she drove the children to school. Susie knew that without a plan at this point she would just come home, pour her coffee and find something to read or watch TV. She needed a plan to follow. The two or three hours previously given over to obsessional thinking had to be filled with something else. Susie and I talked about people she could get to know during this time period and projects she could do that she had been putting off for lack of time. From this we were able to construct a plan that she was willing to try to follow.

Her progress followed the typical pattern—initial success and then some relapses. I held her accountable until her new behavior pattern became more self-rewarding. She began to develop new filters that said, "I can live without the soaps. I will work on real sex with my husband rather than fantasy sex with my books or TV."

We also sought Bill's cooperation. Bill began to reinforce Susie for the positive changes she was making, and he also committed himself to be more sexually responsive to her. This process, though not without its ups and downs, worked. Both Susie and Bill reported that they felt better about themselves and more fulfilled in their marriage. They still had many communication problems to work out, but when the obsession was slowed down Susie had more energy to spend on them.

Susie's story illustrates several behavioral principles that you can employ if you wish to take control of your obsessional thoughts or behaviors. Here are steps you may wish to follow.

1. Identify the undesirable thought or behavior.

2. Reconstruct the series of events or thoughts that lead up to the undesirable thought or behavior.

3. Draw your own chain like the one I drew for Susie.

4. Develop a plan for breaking the chain. In other words, decide on something you can do which will keep you from moving from one link to the next. Remember to start as close to the beginning of the chain as possible.

5. Plan attacks on several links so that if one doesn't work you have a back-up.

6. If you fail, start over again or try at the next attack point.

7. If you succeed, praise God and enjoy your success.

8. Remember that your plan must include substituting thoughts or behavior. (It is hard to stop one behavior or thought unless you have something else to put in its place.)

9. Recruit the help of those around you. They can support you in prayer, hold you accountable, and even fill some of the time previously occupied by the fantasy.

10. Take time to savor your normal sexual contacts.

Opposite-sex friends and spouses are gifts from God. They are not to be used, but enjoyed. Learn to accept them and to receive acceptance from them. This will help you replace obsessional thinking with mature, healthy savoring.

10
Delivering Us from Evil

EVERY CHRISTIAN I HAVE KNOWN who has struggled with obsessional thinking or has fought to overcome temptation has longed to be delivered from the struggle. Even someone as advanced in the faith as the apostle Paul experienced this dilemma. Paul wrote in apparent agony:

I know that nothing good lives in me, that is, in my sinful nature. For I have the desire to do what is good, but I cannot carry it out. For what I do is not the good I want to do; no, the evil I do not want to do—this I keep on doing. Now if I do what I do not want to do, it is no longer I who do it, but it is sin living in me that does it.

So I find this law at work: When I want to do good, evil is

right there with me. For in my inner being I delight in God's law; but I see another law at work in the members of my body, waging war against the law of my mind and making me a prisoner of the law of sin at work within my members. What a wretched man I am! Who will rescue me from this body of death? (Rom 7:18-24)

It is not surprising, then, that Christians who are sexually active in inappropriate ways yearn to be miraculously released from their habits. A relationship with Christ is often offered as a quick cure to those who struggle with sin. People are told that if they receive Christ their sins will "automatically" go away. This is not true. Sins are forgiven and removed, but as long as we live in bodies plagued by the effects of sin we will struggle with sin. Yet God does deliver and heal. The prophet Isaiah shows us how the death of the Messiah makes this possible.

He was despised and rejected by men, a man of sorrows, and familiar with suffering. Like one from whom men hide their faces he was despised, and we esteemed him not. Surely he took up our infirmities and carried our sorrows, yet we considered him stricken by God, smitten by him, and afflicted. But he was pierced for our transgressions, he was crushed for our iniquities; the punishment that brought us peace was upon him, and by his wounds we are healed. We all, like sheep, have gone astray, each of us has turned to his own way; and the LORD has laid on him the iniquity of us all. (Is 53:3-6)

Believing in deliverance and expecting healing are the starting blocks. We need to learn more about the process of deliverance so that we will have realistic expectations and develop a healthy faith. In this chapter we will examine the biblical view of deliverance and discuss practical steps you can take toward experiencing it. We will then look at the need to cooperate with God in the healing process. So often he longs to give us what we long for, but his desires and ours never get on the same wavelength. The more we learn about God and his goodness, the more we will experience the results of our relationship with him—even when we are facing severe temptation.

What Is Deliverance?

The word *deliverance* is used only twice in the New Testament. In both places it has to do with escape. Jesus used it in quoting Isaiah: "He has sent me to proclaim freedom [deliverance] for the prisoners" (Lk 4:18). In Hebrews 11:34 it is used of those who by faith "escaped [were delivered from] the edge of the sword; whose weakness was turned to strength."

In other places in Scripture the idea of deliverance is conveyed by words such as *release* or *rescue,* as in the Romans 7 passage where Paul cries out to be rescued from his struggle with sin.

Oftentimes we get the idea that the person in need of rescue cries out and then waits passively for deliverance to happen. This is not so. Paul's cry in Romans 7 is followed by the wonderful affirmation of victory in chapter 8.

Therefore, there is now no condemnation for those who are in Christ Jesus, because through Christ Jesus the law of the Spirit of life set me free from the law of sin and death. For what the law was powerless to do in that it was weakened by the sinful nature, God did by sending his own Son in the likeness of sinful man to be a sin offering. And so he condemned sin in sinful man, in order that the righteous requirements of the law might be fully met in us, who do not live according to the sinful nature but according to the Spirit. (Rom 8:1-4)

Deliverance is a function of three things: Christ's sacrifice to make it possible, God's power to enable us to be delivered and our willingness to walk in the Spirit. In other words, deliverance does not come automatically with salvation but with obedience; not with justification but with sanctification. It is not usually a once-for-all event, but an everyday process.

Deliverance is a choice or a series of choices that I make. Deliverance from sexual obsession results from choosing to focus on real life and not on fantasy. In Romans 8:5-6 Paul emphasizes that control of the thought process is the key issue: "Those who live according to the sinful nature have their minds set on what that nature desires; but those who live in accordance with the Spirit have their minds set on what the Spirit desires. The mind of sinful man is death, but the mind controlled by the Spirit is life and peace." If we apply verse 5 to sexual thoughts, it might read, "Those who live according to the sinful nature have their minds set on *sexual fantasies and obsessions,* but those who live in accordance with the Spirit have their minds set on *enjoying their sexuality as God intended us to enjoy it.*"

The key issues are faith and obedience: faith that God will meet even our sexual needs and obedience to follow his way by exercising control of our minds. The key to deliverance is found first in being related to God through Christ and then in applying the principle of thought control that we find stressed in Philippians 4:4-9.

You will never practice this principle perfectly. You will never be without sinful thoughts. One thing, however, is certain—if you don't start somewhere, even in an imperfect way, you won't make any progress at all. Trusting God for moment-by-moment deliverance may not be as exciting as some testimonies of immediate release from sin, but it happens to be more the norm of how God works. God rescues a few people almost instantaneously, but most of us are delivered through the process of obedience over time. God longs to stay close to those of us in this latter group in order to keep us from falling. Our weakness can be a wonderful opportunity for fellowship with him if we focus on the opportunity and not just on the problem.

The story of Joseph and the wife of Potiphar, an Egyptian official, is a beautiful example of deliverance in action. In Genesis 39:5-12 we read that after Joseph was put in charge of Potiphar's entire household, God showered his blessings upon it. Because Joseph was handsome and successful he soon found himself in the midst of sexual temptation. Potiphar's wife enticed him to come to bed with her, but Joseph refused. She did not give up easily. Day after day she continued to try to seduce him. Finally, one day, when no one else was in the house, she caught hold of his cloak and said, "Come to bed with me." But he ran out leaving his cloak in her hand.

There is no reason to believe that Potiphar's wife was undesirable or that Joseph was not a normal, virile young man. The temptation was real, and as the seduction went on day after day, Joseph may have cried out for deliverance. He probably said, "God, you know I don't want to mess up, but I do have my limits. I need your help."

Day after day Joseph had to continue to make the right choice. He had to choose to say no. This was important not just because of God's plan to use him in Egypt, but also because he needed the joy of doing the right thing rather than the guilt of failure. Even though Potiphar's wife subsequently accused Joseph of trying to rape her and had him imprisoned, there is no record that he was sorrowful or blamed God. Notice the summary of his prison experience in Genesis 39:20-23:

> While Joseph was there in the prison, the LORD was with him; he showed him kindness and granted him favor in the eyes of the prison warden. So the warden put Joseph in charge of all those held in the prison, and he was made responsible for all that was done there. The warden paid no attention to anything under Joseph's care, because the LORD was with Joseph and gave him success in whatever he did.

Because of his obedience, Joseph was delivered from prison and was used by God to deliver his family from famine. God must have taken care of his sex life too, because Genesis 48 records the heartwarming story of Joseph presenting his sons to his father, Israel, who blessed them.

The most important thing about Joseph's story of deliverance is that he chose to focus on opportunities to do right. It is so easy to become obsessed with possibilities of committing sexual sin. There is, however, an entirely different set of opportunities that can be just as compelling if we allow God to channel us in the right direction. God's plan for us opens up when we follow him. Joseph had faith and a sense of this purpose. He knew that while his brothers meant to harm him by selling him as a slave to Egypt, God used these events to save Joseph and his brothers from the coming famine. As he said to his brothers, "Do not be distressed and do not be angry with yourselves for selling me here, because

... God sent me ahead of you to preserve for you a remnant on earth and to save your lives by a great deliverance" (Gen 45: 5, 7). I wonder if this "great deliverance" would have taken place if Joseph had not been willing to take part in his own deliverance from sexual temptation.

One other aspect of deliverance needs to be stressed: God does not remove evil from us but delivers us from evil. Too many of us have been too naive for too long. We are in the world, and so we are constantly vulnerable to sexual temptation. We cannot act as if temptation doesn't exist, and we dare not take it lightly. We need to focus on growing in faith and trusting God to meet our needs. We also need to focus on developing strong, healthy relationships with those of the opposite sex and strong sexual relationships within marriage if God has given a mate. We should focus on the garden God gives us for our satisfaction, not on someone else's fruit trees or fantasy orchards. Many suffer from sexual starvation because they prefer to wait for the perfect meal rather than savor the good nutritious meal God has provided. In Proverbs 28:19 we read: "He who works his land will have abundant food, but the one who chases fantasies will have his fill of poverty."

Cooperating with God's Healing

Sin always leaves marks, sometimes ugly scars. God wants to heal those scars and restore beauty to life, but his patients—you and I —are not always cooperative. Jesus said, "It is not the healthy who need a doctor, but the sick. But go and learn what this means: 'I desire mercy, not sacrifice.' For I have not come to call the righteous, but sinners" (Mt 9:12-13).

To cooperate with God's plan for restoring wholeness, we need to admit that we are sick. Sexual obsession and choosing to live in a fantasy world are signs of spiritual illness. We need healing, and the doctor wants to help us. He doesn't impose his healing on us, however. As Romans 12:1-2 points out, we are to co-operate in our own healing:

I urge you, brothers, in view of God's mercy, to offer your bodies as living sacrifices, holy and pleasing to God—which is your spiritual worship. Do not conform any longer to the pattern of this world, but be transformed by the renewing of your mind. Then you will be able to test and approve what God's will is—his good, pleasing and perfect will.

This passage shows three ways of cooperating with God: first, by presenting ourselves as living sacrifices; second, by refusing to conform to the world's pattern; and third, by choosing to be transformed by the renewing of our minds. Let's look at these one at a time.

A sacrifice in the Old Testament involved slaying an animal and then presenting it to God as an act of obedience and worship. In Romans God is still calling for obedience and worship but is asking for a living sacrifice. God's pleasure has always been in the living. The picture is clear: he wants us to place ourselves upon the altar and give ourselves totally to him.

Someone has said, "The problem with a living sacrifice is that it keeps crawling off the altar." One minute I may willingly offer myself to God, and the next minute I may willfully creep away But if I want healing, I must get back on the altar. God doesn't focus on where we have been. He just encourages us to stay where he can help us.

The second way to cooperate with God is to refuse to conform to the world. We don't avoid the quicksand of the world by blissfully skipping through the woods. We must choose our path carefully. I must not be afraid to ask myself if a certain path is the one I really want to take, or if I am just following it because I think I can't resist the pressures of a "liberated" society.

Conformity is not always black and white. Sometimes it subtly sneaks up on us. It often begins by trying to listen to two stations at once. In the fall of the year I like to keep up with my favorite college football teams. If possible I will try to listen to them on the radio by switching from one station to another. Invariably, however, I will become engrossed in one game and forget the other. As Christians we can get so interested in the world that we fail to tune back to God. We may not intend to conform to the world but we do so by quietly dropping our interest in God's station. Cooperation with God by refusing to conform to the world requires discipline and commitment.

The third way to cooperate is to choose to be transformed. This is powerful and exciting, and yet this may be what we most try to avoid. Change, even change in a positive direction, frightens most of us. The Greek word Paul uses for *transformed* is the root of our word *metamorphosis*. It is the word used to describe the process by which caterpillars are changed into beautiful butterflies. I don't know why we sometimes choose to stay in our dark cocoons, but we do. God is waiting for us to cooperate with him so he can unfold our beauty and our power to fly—qualities he has placed in us which remain hidden and untapped as long as we remain in the cocoon.

We cooperate with God when we allow him to transform us. This begins with our thoughts. He wants us to focus on him, not our sin. Our minds are renewed by our quiet times, the times we spend soaking up who God is and what he wants to do with us.

Healing will be accomplished when I add my part to what God is already doing. He doesn't mind renewing us. He just doesn't choose to help us without our willingness and cooperation.

Attitudes That Make Healing Possible
As I have worked with numerous people at different stages of growth toward wholeness, I have discovered attitudes that seem to be essential if deliverance and healing are to take place, if one is to escape the tyranny of boredom that surrounds sexual sin. Let me summarize these attitudes here so you can evaluate your own readiness to be healed.

The first essential attitude is *openness*. I must be open and vulnerable to God and my fellow Christians. It is time to stop playing games of deceit, denial and perfectionism and admit that I am a broken person in need of healing. Ideally, this openness will be met with acceptance, prayerful concern and a call to accountability. If you need help or healing it may seem hard to find an accepting body of believers, but you must start somewhere. If you keep your door closed and double-bolted, there is no possibility of hope. Often the acceptance you feel from a single individual with whom you have been honest will open the door to further healing from God through others.

Over and over again I have stressed the *willingness to be remolded*. What more can I say? Without willingness, healing will not take place. Jim came to see me three different times in two years. Each time he was more depressed and in worse shape physically. I invited him to open up to me and to deal with the issues that disturbed him. He wasn't willing. He chose to continue pursuing his sexual fantasies. He admitted that his life had no meaning but refused to take the necessary steps toward healing.

Closely related to willingness is *obedience*. Once I say yes to God in the general sense (willingness), I will then be asked to say yes to him in the specific sense (obedience). Once I realize what God wants me to do, I have to choose to do it. Once I realize what God does not want me to do, I have to choose not to do it. Obedience is a habit that is developed as we obey in one situation and then another. Each time we obey, it becomes easier. Often the habit of obedience is not nearly so painful as the thought of no longer following all our own desires. Obedience brings blessing, but that is hard to remember when we are sexually tempted.

Finally, we need an *awareness of God's care*. I could not have written this book without a strong belief that God actively works on behalf of those who are caught in the world of sexual obsession. Such people often say to themselves, "I can't do anything! God must have forsaken me." Here is a good place to practice thought substitution. Repeat Philippians 4:13: "I can do everything through him who gives me strength." We have hope because forgiveness for our failures is available and because God is personally invested in our success. This is an exciting alternative to sexual insanity. Take heart from the Scriptures! "For everything that was written in the past was written to teach us, so that through endurance and the encouragement of the Scriptures we might have hope. . . . May the God of hope fill you with all joy and peace as you trust in him, so that you may overflow with hope by the power of the Holy Spirit" (Rom 15:4, 13).

II
Enjoying Sexual Sanity

SOME OF YOU WHO ARE READING this book may feel that certain sexual behaviors which I have described as inappropriate are normal and even healthy for you. But both *normal* and *healthy* can be quite subjective concepts. I would choose to say instead that sex is intended to fill a particular role in our lives, and that the closer we come to that role, the greater the probability that we will enjoy sound mental and physical health.

Normal sexuality by my definition is not determined statistically by the number of people who engage in specific sexual practices. If it were, sexual obsession could become the norm. Instead, normality is defined by what the Bible has to say about sexuality. You may not like this point of view but, if you are honest, you may recognize that your present position is not entirely satisfying either.

Volumes have been written about biblical sexuality, and I am not trying to duplicate their findings. My purpose is to outline a basic approach to sexuality which can serve as a model. Such a model may be useful for those struggling with sexual obsession. It may also be useful for those who are becoming sexually aware and trying to make sound decisions about what to do with their feelings.

Pleasure and Procreation
The first scriptural affirmation about sexuality is that it is created by God. Genesis 1:27 states, "Male and female he created them." Many find it easier to believe that God created the capacity for sex than that he is also the inventor of sexual intercourse and erotic feelings. Somehow we feel that Satan must have devised the pleasurable aspects of sex. Such is not the case.

Sex was created by God for both pleasure and procreation. In his helpful book *Intended for Pleasure,* Dr. Ed Wheat writes: "Please keep one tremendous fact in view: God himself invented sex for our delight. It was his gift to us—intended for pleasure."[1] Genesis 2:24-25 makes it clear that there was to be no shame associated with the husband-wife relationship: "A man will leave his father and mother and be united to his wife, and they will become one flesh. The man and his wife were both naked, and they felt no shame." Undoubtedly sexual pleasure was part of the blissful experience which God intended for Adam and Eve in the Garden of Eden.

Not only did God create sex in its erotic form, but he also created it for woman's pleasure as well as man's. The female capacity for sexual arousal and orgasmic activity is great. Without question God designed female sexual response as a part of what it means to be truly female. We violate God's plan if we emphasize pleasure for the male without helping him realize his responsibility to carefully consider his spouse's pleasure needs.

The New Testament clarifies the mutual responsibility of husband and wife in 1 Corinthians 7:2-5. This passage definitely supports the validity of the erotic aspects of sex. Paul says, "Do not deprive each other." Deprive one another of what? Affection and pleasure. Paul also emphasizes that sex is for both the male and the female. God created it that way. Normal sexuality recognizes the importance of this egalitarian sexual relationship.

Procreation, the privilege of bringing a new life into the world, is also one of the greatest gifts God has given to us. This experience has been viewed as the closest we may come to immortality. We live on through the lives we have brought into the world. In his great wisdom God chose to link together the celebration of husband and wife belonging to each other and providing pleasure for each other with the possibility of new life. Christian sexuality is all about life, new life through sharing physical pleasure in the security of a committed relationship. Procreation and pleasure are two of the greatest celebrations of life. Understanding the joys of procreation opens the door to greater appreciation of the joys of erotic love in marriage.

Enjoyment in the Relationship

It is reasonable to think that where there is physical union there should also be psychological union. If the bodies of the husband and wife belong to each other, as Paul states, one would hope that a married couple could develop a deep emotional attachment for each other along with the physical attraction. Unfortunately many couples report that this never happens.

One frustrated wife said, "My husband is a stranger. He only comes to me when he expects me to make love." What a pity! I believe that the deeper the emotional ties, the greater the possibility of developing the physical relationship. What is making love if not expressing physically the depths of emotional feelings? Having sexual intercourse may or may not be making love. That depends on the relationship.

One reason sexual fidelity makes sense is that it allows the emotional relationship to grow so that the physical relationship can be fully enjoyed. God intends that husband and wife belong only to each other and that they celebrate the joys of their unique relationship by enjoying their sexual life together.

Why limit sex to marriage? If it is so great, why not experience it at all stages of life with as many partners as possible? My answer is clear. When sexuality is used in this way it loses its greatness. Sexuality within marriage is intended to maximize the value and self-esteem of each spouse. It is designed to say, "You are wonderful; you are exciting; you are unique; you are you. I love you and you are mine."

Sex outside of the marriage relationship always has qualifiers which either dilute the experience or in many cases change sexual intercourse for what God intended to something far less. That something less is often pleasure without person. We become machines rather than unique beings made in God's image. When sex stops saying, "You are special," it says you are disposable.

A Creative Process

The sex act is erroneously referred to in American folklore as "doin' what comes naturally." The belief that sex is instinctive traps many people. If it is instinctive, these people think, then all who participate must immediately be experts.

Nothing could be further from the truth. Most young couples quickly learn just how unnatural some aspects of making love are. For example, it is natural to seek pleasure for yourself. It may feel unnatural to give pleasure to another. Even talking about what is pleasurable for your spouse is very unnatural for many people.

I firmly believe that God intended sex to be a creative process which lasts a lifetime as couples continually grow in their relationship and change in their awareness of their sexual needs. Sandy and I have found it helpful to view our sex life as a process of learning to be lovers rather than as a performance that we are somehow supposed to know how to give. This view has helped us replace the pressure of wanting to be good lovers with the pleasure of learning together. We seek to learn to relate, to give pleasure, to receive pleasure and, most of all, to respect each other in the delicate creative process.

When we view sex as a creative process rather than just repetition of yesterday's behaviors, we protect ourselves against boredom. Machinelike sex inevitably becomes boring, and the participants often turn to sexual obsession as a means of trying to escape the boredom. On the other hand, when we see sex as a creative act with a loving and accepting spouse, the excitement may remain for a lifetime.

Creative sex leaves room for seriousness as well as humor. It also allows for excitement, novelty and surprise. When you experience these aspects of sex, the biblical admonition "Do not deprive each other" makes a lot of sense. Why deprive one another of something that can be so wonderful?

Sex is like a good meal—it is intended to be savored and enjoyed with your closest friend, your spouse. Too often, however, it is as if we are stuffing down a Thanksgiving dinner, we take as much pleasure as we can, as fast as we can, and then we become obsessed with what is coming next. Is it any wonder we become bored?

Controlling habits is never easy. Especially those habits which are formed out of our desires for pleasure and gratification. So what? Who says life is going to be easy. My point is that sex is too beautiful a gift to be wasted by allowing ourselves to become enmeshed in unproductive or destructive habits. After twenty-five years of marriage, Sandy and I find special joy in hearing one of the children say, "I suppose you are going into the bedroom to kiss." Our response is simple, "Why not? It is God's gift to us, a gift to last a lifetime."

Notes

Chapter 1: Sanity in an Insane World
[1]Lawrence C. Kolb, *Modern Clinical Psychiatry,* 9th ed. (Philadelphia: W. B. Saunders, 1977), p. 145.
[2]Calvin Miller, *The Valiant Papers* (Grand Rapids: Zondervan Publishing House, 1982), p. 66.

Chapter 2: The Not-So-Modern Crises in Values
[1]Mohr & Associates, *Pedophilia and Exhibitionism* (Toronto: University of Toronto Press, 1964), p. 25.
[2]John Allan Lavender, *Your Marriage Needs Three Love Affairs* (Denver: Accent Books, 1978), pp. 104-5.
[3]Dennis Guernsey, *Thoroughly Married* (Waco, Tex.: Word Books, 1977), pp. 61-62.
[4]Sandra Kahn and Jean Davis, *The Kahn Report on Sexual Preferences* (New York: St. Martin's Press, 1981), p. 30.
[5]Gay Talese, *Thy Neighbor's Wife* (New York: Dell, 1980), pp. 178-79.
[6]Lewis B. Smedes, *Sex for Christians* (Grand Rapids: Eerdmans, 1976), pp. 43-44.
[7]Helen Singer Kaplan, *The New Sex Therapy* (New York: Brunner/Mazel Publications, 1974), p. 159.
[8]John White, *Eros Defiled* (Downers Grove, Ill.: InterVarsity Press, 1977), pp. 10-11.
[9]J. LoPiccolo and L. LoPiccolo, eds., *Handbook of Sex Therapy* (New York: Plenum Press, 1978), p. 6.
[10]Kaplan, *The New Sex Therapy,* pp. 126-32.

Chapter 3: How We Are Aroused
[1]Robert Stoller, *Perversion: The Erotic Form of Hatred* (New York: Pantheon Books, 1975), p. 6.
[2]Smedes, *Sex for Christians,* p. 78.
[3]Ibid., p. 79.
[4]Paul A. Hauck, *How to Do What You Want to Do* (Philadelphia: Westminster Press, 1976), p. 28.
[5]Marabel Morgan, *The Total Woman* (Old Tappan, N. J.: Fleming H. Revell, 1973).
[6]R. E. Love, L. R. Sloan and M. J. Schmidt, "Viewing Pornography and Sex Guilt: The Priggish, the Prudent, and the Profligate," *Journal of Consulting and Clinical Psychology* 44 (1976): 624-29.
[7]Kaplan, *The New Sex Therapy,* p. 125.

Chapter 4: Obsession: The Vicious Cycle
[1]Kolb, *Modern Clinical Psychiatry,* p. 145.
[2]John T. Watkins, "The Rational-Emotive Dynamics of Impulsive Disorders" in Albert Ellis and Russell Grieger, *Handbook of Rational-Emotive Therapy* (New York: Springer, 1977), p. 135.
[3]Ibid., pp. 136-37.

Chapter 5: Masturbation, Voyeurism, Promiscuity
[1]James Leslie McCary, *McCary's Human Sexuality,* 3d ed. (New York: D. Van Nostrand, 1978), p. 150.
[2]Dwight Small, *Christian, Celebrate Your Sexuality* (Old Tappan, N.J.: Fleming H. Revell, 1974), pp. 75-76.
[3]Norman Geisler, *Ethics: Alternatives and Issues* (Grand Rapids: Zondervan, 1971).
[4]White, *Eros Defiled,* p. 45.
[5]Ibid., p. 36.
[6]V. Mary Stewart, *Sexual Freedom* (Downers Grove, Ill.: InterVarsity Press, 1974)
[7]McCary, *Human Sexuality,* p. 362.
[8]Stewart, *Sexual Freedom,* p. 13.

Chapter 6: Pornography and Personal Identity
[1]Rollo May, *Love and Will* (New York: Dell, 1969), p. 44.
[2]Ibid., p. 56.
[3]Paul A. Hauck, *Overcoming Worry* (Philadelphia: Westminster Press, 1975), pp. 17-18.
[4]Earl D. Wilson, *The Undivided Self* (Downers Grove, Ill.: InterVarsity Press, 1983).
[5]Karl Menninger, *Whatever Became of Sin?* (New York: Hawthorn Books, 1973), p. 17.
[6]Talese, *Thy Neighbor's Wife,* p. 394.
[7]May, *Love and Will,* p. 45.

Chapter 7: Homosexuality
[1]David Field, *The Homosexual Way—A Christian Option?* (Downers Grove, Ill.: InterVarsity Press, 1979), p. 30.
[2]John Money and Claus Wiedeking, "Gender Identity Role," in Benjamin B. Wolman and John Money, eds., *Handbook of Human Sexuality* (Englewood Cliffs, N.J.: Prentice-Hall, 1980), p. 282.
[3]Ibid., p. 281.
[4]Gerald Davison, "Homosexuality and the Ethics of Behavioral Intervention," *Journal of Homosexuality,* Spring 1977.
[5]E. Mansell Pattison and Myrna Loy Pattison, " 'Ex-Gays': Religiously Mediated Change in Homosexuals," *American Journal of Psychiatry* 137, no. 12 (Dec. 1980): 1553.
[6]Alan Bell, Indiana Study reprinted in Portland *Oregonian.* August 25, 1981.

Chapter 8: Facing Temptation
[1]Hauck, *How to Do What You Want to Do,* pp. 75-76.
[2]Phillip Swihart, *How to Live with Your Feelings* (Downers Grove, Ill.: InterVarsity Press, 1976), pp. 19-20.

Chapter 11: Enjoying Sexuality Sanity
[1]Ed Wheat, *Intended for Pleasure* (Old Tappan, N. J.: Fleming H. Revell, 1977), p. 10.